M000202081

Stones of Remembrance

Dr. Fuchsia T. Pickett

Charisma
HOUSE

STONES OF REMEMBRANCE by Dr. Fuchsia T. Pickett
Published by Charisma House
A part of Strang Communications Company
600 Rinehart Road
Lake Mary, Florida 32746
www.charismahouse.com

Unless otherwise noted, all Scripture quotations are from the
King James Version of the Bible.

Scripture quotations marked NIV are from the Holy Bible, New
International Version. Copyright © 1973, 1978, 1984,
International Bible Society. Used by permission.

Library of Congress Cataloging-in-Publication Data
Pickett, Fuchsia T.
    Stones of remembrance / Fuchsia T. Pickett
       p. cm.
    Includes bibliographical references.
    ISBN: 0-88419-538-4 (pbk.)
    1. Pickett, Fuchsia T. 2. Pentecostals—United States—
Biography. 3. Evangelists—United States—Biography.
4. Private revelations. 5. Visions. 6. Shekinah Church
Ministries (Blountville, Tenn.)
I. Title.
BX8762.Z8P536 1998
289.9'4'092—dc21   98-9320
[B]   CIP

01 02 03 04   9 8 7 6 5
Printed in the United States of America

Contents

Introduction

I GIVE ALL THE honor and glory to God for what is shared on the following pages. It is important to me for the reader to understand one thing. I had no intention to write my life story. It was not in my plans, present or future.

But a trusted friend and respected prophet, Dr. David Schoch, and I were ministering in Alabama together. As we arrived at the church one morning, he met me at the car and said, "Fuchsia, I want to say something to you."

"All right," I said.

"Let's go in and sit down in the sanctuary."

We sat in the back of the sanctuary before anyone else had arrived, and Dr. David Schoch looked me straight in the eye and said very seriously, "I want you to write your life story."

Immediately I remonstrated, lifting both hands as if to wave them toward his face, responding *no* as emphatically as I could. "I don't have anything to write about Fuchsia Pickett. I don't have a life story to tell about me. All I have is what God has done for me."

Then David changed his approach and said, "I am not talking to you just as a friend. This is a word from the Lord for you. You are to write your life story. The fact that you feel as if you don't have one is the reason you can write it honestly and sincerely." Without allowing me to interrupt he continued, "This generation has a right to know people who have experienced what you have experienced in God. They read about Maria Woodworth-Etter, Katherine Kuhlman, Smith Wigglesworth, and others from other generations . . ."

"Wait a minute," I interrupted. "I am not one of them. I am not in the category with any of those people."

He responded, "This generation of people has a right to know what has happened in their lifetime through lives who have touched God's supernatural power and revelation. I want you to write about your 'Teacher.' They have a right to know how your 'Teacher'—the precious Holy Spirit—has taught you."

Having heard the authoritative tone of the prophet, I was more willing to discuss my reservations about such a project. I said, "Brother Schoch, I have always felt that the Lord revealed Himself to me in these visitations of the Spirit because I was so dumb I could not receive His truth without explicit explanation. Because of my theological background, which kept me ignorant of the moving of the Holy Spirit in His gifts and manifestations of power, I felt that when I received the Pentecostal experience, the Holy Spirit had to 'catch me up' to those who already understood His ways better than I."

During those first years, as I shared some of those precious experiences, there were a few traditional Pentecostal pastors who felt that people should not be encouraged to seek "experiences." They felt I should not be teaching people to seek experiences, but to seek God and study His Word, and He would reveal Himself to them. But because of a reprimand from a senior minister who was in a leadership position, I decided to lock these precious revelatory experiences up inside, and I did not share them for years. Only after establishing our Bible college at Fountaingate Ministries in Plano, Texas, would I share parts of these supernatural visitations with my students. But I did not share them publicly because of the objections I had experienced years earlier.

When I expressed this reservation to Dr. Schoch, his simple response was, "It is not that way now. It is God's time to share your story. I do not feel you will exalt yourself in sharing those glorious times. They belong to the body of Christ—they are not just yours, but for this generation."

Later I talked with Dr. Judson Cornwall, my senior pastor and friend, and told him all Dr. Schoch had said. He listened carefully to me. I pleaded with him, "Judson, please hear me. I don't want to write anything that is going to exalt me. If I can share what God has shown me without it exalting me, I will do it."

He responded kindly, "You write it, Sis, and I

promise you I will go over it with a fine-tooth comb to see if there is anything in it that exalts Fuchsia Pickett. If there is, I will edit it out."

Finally, I talked with my publisher as I submitted my latest manuscript to them. As he talked to me about writing more, I said cautiously, "You might not want to print my next book."

"What is it?" he asked curiously.

"It is to be about my life—encounters I have had with God and my Teacher as He has taught me."

"We want it," he replied, smiling.

"All right," I acquiesced.

There seemed to be nothing more to protest. My reservations were put away by my dear friends, and my publisher felt it was time for my story. So I prepared my notes and accepted the kind invitation of Joy Strang to bring a few friends to their family's mountain home and, in that comfortable setting, in the presence of those ten special, precious people, I related these experiences to them. We rejoiced at the personal but profound ministry of the Holy Spirit.

Brother Schoch wrote me a note when he realized the arrangements were forthcoming to publish my story. "My heart has been singing a new song since I heard you were beginning to write your story for posterity and the generations to come. I am committed to your doing that. I believe it is of God."

So I dedicate these pages to the Joshua generation that I believe will possess "the land." I trust they will come to know, through my testimony as well as through the testimony of others, that God is faithful to teach and to reveal Himself through His Word when we choose to seek Him with all our hearts. ∾

One

Memorial Stones

J UST TWO YEARS ago as I was still wondering how I would put my story together, I heard the Holy Spirit whisper to me, "Stones of remembrance."

He caught my attention, and I wondered what He was saying. My mind went immediately to Scripture for an explanation, knowing that all true revelation must stand the test of Scripture.

What did the Bible have to say about stones? I remembered then that when the children of Israel crossed over the Jordan River into the Promised Land of Canaan, they were commanded by the Lord to "take up twelve stones from the middle of the Jordan from right where the priests stood and to carry them over with you and put them down at the place where you stay tonight" (Josh. 4:3, NIV).

Each priest took up one stone from the middle of

the river, twelve in all, for each of the twelve tribes. When all the people had crossed over, Joshua set up the twelve stones they had taken out of the Jordan and said to the Israelites:

> In the future when your descendants ask their fathers, "What do these stones mean?" tell them, "Israel crossed the Jordan on dry ground." For the LORD your God dried up the Jordan before you until you had crossed over. The LORD your God did to the Jordan just what he had done to the Red Sea when he dried it up before us until we had crossed over. He did this so that all the peoples of the earth might know that the hand of the LORD is powerful and so that you might always fear the LORD your God.
>
> —JOSHUA 4:21–24, NIV

It was important to the Lord that the children of Israel make a memorial so that future generations who had not experienced the power of God in the drying up of the Jordan River could understand and fear the Lord. As I pondered that fact, I began to understand that the supernatural experiences I had enjoyed were not just for me to receive revelation of God's wonderful truths but to leave them for others who would follow as well.

As I shared these revelations with a small group of friends during a retreat planned for this purpose, I heard the Holy Spirit say to me, "Now you are laying the stones. When I sent you out as a mother in Israel, I placed a mandate on your life to go to the body of Christ and look for leaders to help them prepare to go into the land of their inheritance.

These are not just personal experiences. They are stones of revelation that will help people who come behind to understand the ways of God as you were helped to understand them." For years I had seen, heard, and declared about the mighty river of God—the revival we were going to experience.

The Scriptures teach the power of testimony. In the Book of Revelation we read, "And they overcame him by the blood of the Lamb, and by the word of their testimony; and they loved not their lives unto the death" (Rev. 12:11). The revelations of God's truth to me that I will share in this book as memorial stones are my testimony of how God, in His great mercy and loving-kindness to me, shined His light on the truth of the Word to open my understanding to His ways.

The memorial stones that Joshua laid were placed in the water at the place where the Israelites crossed over into their inheritance. They were placed there as a testimony to the generation that would come behind them. When Dr. David Schoch gave me the word of the Lord to write this book, he said emphatically, "You have to write it because there is a generation coming behind you that needs to know your testimony of how God revealed Himself to you."

PROCESS OF REVELATION

REVELATION IS AN "unveiling" of Christ. It is the work of the Holy Spirit to teach us, to reveal Jesus to us, and fulfill the Christ life in and through us.

As we open our lives to receive the truth of the Word of God, there is a divine process, a working of the Holy Spirit in our minds and hearts, to bring us to the unveiling of Christ.

There is no true revelation of God apart from the Word of God. The Holy Spirit has been given the task of unveiling Christ—the living Word—in us through the application of the truth of the written Word to our lives. The written Word works in us a divine process of revelation that changes our lives. This process includes seven steps.[1]

1. Information

The first step toward revelation in this divine process is to receive *information*. We must first receive a basic truth in our minds and hearts in order for the Holy Spirit to bring it to our remembrance. We cannot expect this first step toward revelation to happen apart from spending time daily reading and meditating on the Word of God. When our nation was first founded, the Bible was the textbook used in our schools. Our children were taught the Scriptures as soon as they learned to read. They learned the Ten Commandments and studied the Old Testament patriarchs as well as the parables of Jesus. What a wonderful foundation those generations were given of the principles of God.

Today our children's minds are filled with worldly information, and many have never heard of the Old Testament patriarchs. They have not been given the opportunity to receive the information—the basic truth—of the Scriptures.

As Christians we need to spend time reading and memorizing the Word of God and teaching our children to do likewise. This is the first step in making it possible for the Holy Spirit to do His wonderful work of bringing us divine revelation.

Joshua received a mandate that would guarantee

his success—to meditate day and night on the law of God (Josh. 1:8). How faithfully we follow this same mandate will determine our success or failure in walking toward true revelation. Without a knowledge of the information contained in the Scriptures, we cannot have a fuller revelation of Christ within us, even if we are born-again Christians.

2. ILLUMINATION

Have you enjoyed the experience of reading a familiar passage of Scripture and suddenly having a light come on in your mind? You see how a principle applies to an area of your life, or perhaps you see why God responded to a person's plight in Scripture the way He did. In that moment information has taken on another dimension—illumination.

When information begins to be a light to our spirits, it becomes *illumination.* In ways we never understood before, we understand the truth we are reading that was once only information to us. At that point it becomes our responsibility to walk in obedience to that truth.

3. INSPIRATION

As the Holy Spirit continues His process of bringing revelation to us, we find ourselves responding to the truth with His joy. The Holy Spirit receives the Word with joy, and as we receive it from Him, it becomes *inspiration* to us. New desires to obey the Word fill our hearts.

Inspiration makes us hungry for the Word of God. The divine work of the Holy Ghost makes us "hunger and thirst after righteousness" (Matt. 5:6). No person can make us hungry for the Word. If we find ourselves hungering for truth, we are receiving a new invitation from the Holy Spirit to receive greater revelation.

People who sit in church and are bored to death with the preached Word are not hungry. We will eat anything when we are hungry. The Scriptures declare that "the full soul loatheth an honeycomb; but to the hungry soul every bitter thing is sweet" (Prov. 27:7). When we are hungry for the Word, we are saying we want more of God. The blessed Holy Spirit then splits the veil of our darkened minds, emotions, and wills, and that part of Jesus which enters our ears becomes life on the inside.

4. NEW REVELATION

The written Word of God (*logos*) can be viewed as a transcription of God's voice. When the transcribed Word moves from our heads to our hearts, inspiring us to its reality, it becomes a living Word to us (*rhema*). That living Word is *revelation*.

Revelation makes the truth become a living Person to us. As we respond to the revelation of that divine Person, we yield our wills, minds, and emotions to His divine character of holiness and righteousness, and the life of Christ is unveiled within us. When the Holy Spirit breathes a revealed truth into our spirits, it becomes our life. We actually experience what we had previously heard only as information.

It is our obedience to the revelation we receive that enables the Holy Spirit to keep giving us new revelation. *Once revelation begins to flow in us, it keeps flowing unless we resist it.* It is a serious matter indeed to disobey divine revelation that has come to our hearts. Darkness is dispelled only by the light that pierces it. If we give place to darkness rather than walking in the light we have received, we will suffer the consequences of our disobedience.

5. REALIZATION

After revelation begins to work in our heart, the next step in the divine growth process is *realization*. Realization is the recognition that we are being changed through our obedience to the revelation that has become a part of our lives. We realize that the change that is taking place in us is reality. It affects the way we live.

We don't know exactly what happened, but we realize we are not losing our tempers like we used to. We realize we are walking in a grace we did not have before. Other people can observe this change in us. Our spirits are sensitive to the truth that has become a living reality in us, and we are careful not to disobey it.

6. TRANSFORMATION

Transformation of our character occurs as we allow death to come to the self-life through the rending of the veil of flesh. Those deep, inward tendencies to self-centeredness and lack of love that reside in our natural man are fundamentally changed—transformed—into holy desires and the love of Christ for others. The life of Christ can then be lived through us in the world.

A consistent walk in greater depths of revelation brings a gradual *transformation* to our lives. We are changed from glory to glory into the image of the Son through our obedience to the revelation we receive.

7. MANIFESTATION

The final step the Spirit of Truth works in us is the *manifestation* of Jesus' character in our lives. Maturity is the beauty of Jesus as it is seen in the people who have allowed revelation to touch their lives in every area of their souls and spirits. In obedience to God they have continually turned from sin and allowed the nature of Christ to be fully unveiled in them.

The beautiful part of the process of revelation is that different truth may be at different stages in us at the same time. One truth may be at the fourth stage— that of revelation—becoming a reality to us and preparing us to move on to realization and transformation. Another truth we have just received as information may inspire us to seek God for revelation. In this way, as we consistently avail ourselves of the reading and hearing of the Word, the Holy Spirit takes the Book and writes it on our hearts.

Information is transferring my notes to your mind. It has no eternal value unless it goes beyond that. But in our search for wisdom, we pray that God will make His Word real to us and open our minds to receive divine revelation. It was the Son of God Himself who declared in the face of the tempter, "Man shall not live by bread alone, but by every word that proceedeth out of the mouth of God" (Matt. 4:4). It is God's proceeding Word that contains the power to save our souls. (See James 1:21.)

True revelation of God cannot be found in seeking "experiences." He has chosen to reveal Himself to us through His written Word. Any experience that we call supernatural must be judged by the authority of the written Word and must never violate any principle that is revealed therein.

My walk with God for seventeen years <u>before</u> I received the baptism of the Holy Spirit was given to the study of the Word of God. The knowledge I had, though somewhat faulty, was the foundation upon which the Holy Spirit could teach, clarify, and correct my understanding of God. Sometimes He chose to do that through visions or divinely inspired conversations with Him. Other times He simply shined His light into my heart through the written Word, and I understood what I had not understood before.

The test of true revelation is the power it has to transform our thinking and our lives to the image of Christ. Our sinful nature is changed into the character of Christ as we choose to allow the Word of God to split the veil of flesh within us and reveal the incorruptible seed of Christ. His life is allowed to mature in us through our choices to obey His Word as it is revealed to our hearts.

Our wonderful Teacher, the Holy Spirit, can speak to us in many ways to bring the light of the Word to our darkened minds. It is then our responsibility to embrace the truth and turn from sin and our sinful nature to walk in that light. As we choose to live daily in the light of the Word, we will find ourselves swimming in the river of revelation that is coming from the throne of God.

And that river will flow through our lives to others who come behind, making us a part of the great End-Time harvest of souls that is coming. I am excited to be a part of that End-Time revival. With this book I am laying the stones of remembrance in order. I am going on into the land of my inheritance to conquer the "ites" and bring the spoils of the kingdom to my heart and life. I am endeavoring to help God's people enter the land of their inheritance that they have never possessed. I believe we will not "marry" the "ites" this time, but we will possess the land and conquer all its former inhabitants.

In the process we will see the church of Christ become what the Father has intended for her to become—a glorious church without spot or wrinkle—rejoicing as we enter into the "greater works" ministry Jesus promised us and watching the kingdom of God established in the earth.

God is declaring that He is going to do a new thing in the earth. I remember the night He whispered to me, "You will live to see it come in." I am expecting to go on into the inheritance that is ordained for the church. I have laid the stones of memorial for where I have been. But I am not staying here. I want to help the church go into Canaan, the land of promise, and I long to help others go into their inheritance. There is land to be possessed; there is a deliverance coming. And we are going into the land to conquer the "ites."

As you read this book, allow the divine process of revelation to change your life. Step into the flow—plunge into the river until you are swimming in the river of revelation that is coming from the throne of God. God is going to send a revival that will rout the enemies of our souls and let the church receive her inheritance. I believe there will not just be blessings and miracles in the coming revival, but holiness and righteousness as well as the church becomes prepared to meet her King. ∿

Two

Early Memories

I N A LITTLE rural area called Irishburg, part of the Axton, Virginia, community, in Henry County near Martinsville, Virginia, I was the second of four children born to Monroe and Fannie Hundley Turner. I had three brothers: Morton, Melvin, and Everette. Only Everette survived to adulthood, and we have walked the narrow road of faith together until his homegoing a few years ago.

My maternal grandparents, William and Angeline Hundley, were lovely people who owned a large plantation in Virginia. I have fond memories of visiting my grandparents' home as a little girl, roaming in the large fruit orchards, surveying the vast fields of crops, and entertaining myself with the many farm animals who made their home there. I was fascinated by the cows, horses, pigs, chickens, and other creatures of the farm.

The large, white plantation house was intriguing with the many lightning rods that protruded from its roof. I had never seen anything like that before, and, as I was quite an inquisitive child, I asked my parents about the strange things coming out of Grandma and Grandpa's roof. They patiently explained their purpose to my young mind.

There were a number of tenant homes on this large farm. They were beautiful little houses that surrounded the large farmhouse. I remember the excitement I felt when we turned down the long road leading from the highway to this beautiful place. It was always such a joy for me to get to spend time with these special grandparents, William and Angeline Hundley.

My parents settled in a community called Beckam, several miles from this home place. I retain my earliest childhood memories from our life in Beckam. Daddy and Mother were faithful church attenders. My mother played the pump organ sometimes when the regular organist was not present. The pastor of the Beckam Methodist Church was a circuit rider. He was often a guest in our home during his stay in our area. I remember what a sensation he created when he taught my mother to cook fried tomatoes, something that was unusual for us.

It was here that I remember receiving my first spanking. Two of my nieces had come to visit us one Sunday afternoon to go to the Sunday afternoon church service with us. We were dressed for church in our pretty Sunday clothes when we decided to slide down the bank in our front yard that was damp beneath the sand. You can imagine what fun we had and what a mess we made of our pretty clothes. Soon our parents came to inspect the squeals and laughter and to bring "order" to our unruliness.

When I was nearly five years old, a severe hailstorm tore into our entire community and laid all our crops flat to the ground. Shortly after that, my parents moved our family to Leaksville, North Carolina. Many years later this little community would merge with two others (Spray and Draper) to become the city of Eden, North Carolina, and it remains that today.

My brother Everette was one year and twenty-seven days older than I. But I was the larger child, a chubby, blond-haired tot, while he had a darker complexion and was the curly headed, cute one. When it came time to enroll him in school, the first-grade teacher came by our home to visit. I was standing in the yard watching her approach our house, and I heard her ask my parents why I was not in school. My mother explained that although I was larger than my brother I was only five years old. (There were no kindergartens at that time.) I would not turn six until December 29. The teacher told my parents to go ahead and enroll me in school. So Everette and I started school together in the same class at the Leaksville grade school.

My parents believed in strict discipline of their children, teaching us respect for our elders, while at the same time showing love to us. My mother was the most philanthropic person I ever knew. The greatest joy of her life was to give to people—sometimes from what she had and often from what she bought especially for them. She was a giver as long as she lived.

My mother was a faithful Methodist whose service for the church ranged from carrying flowers weekly from her own garden to the sanctuary to presiding as president of the Women's Missionary Society. She came to a personal relationship with Jesus at a Methodist camp meeting in High Point, North Carolina.

My papa was a strong teacher in our home. Papa taught us how to live. He taught us the principles of truthfulness and integrity that molded our lives, as well as practical knowledge. When I started school I already knew my alphabet, having learned it on my father's knee. He taught me how to lace and tie my shoes and, using broken broom straws from the hearth, taught me to spell my name and "write" my numbers by making the broken straws form the letters of the alphabet and numbers.

Papa's sense of integrity was imparted to his children in very practical ways. I remember when we were sledding in the winter, he let us know that we did not deserve to jump on the sled and ride down the hill if we had not helped to pull the sled up the long, snow-covered hill. He did not tolerate childrens' "fibs." One of the greatest principles he instilled into the fiber of my being was to tell the truth and to keep my word when I had committed to do something. These have been basic guiding factors in my life to this day. Truth was a foundational stone in the character of my life.

I graduated from the Leaksville high school at sixteen years of age as the youngest student, yet quite mature for my age. Those were good years. I was reared in a protected environment and prepared for the life that God had ordained for me, though I still did not know Him personally. ༄

Three

Longing for Relationship With God

ⷮ

I WAS ROCKED IN A Methodist cradle and reared in a Methodist home. Though I went to church from the time I was a baby and grew up in a very honest, good, moral home, I didn't know anything about being born again. Even as a young woman I didn't know Jesus as my Savior.

My parents saw to it that I was in church and Sunday school every week. I sang in the choir. As a nine-year-old girl, I was the youngest girl ever invited to represent the women's missionary society of the United Methodist Church (M.E. Church South). That honor, bestowed largely because of my mother's involvement as president of the women's missionary society, came to me again as a thirteen-year-old girl, when I stood in that position once again at Brevard College.

I remember wanting to know God from the time I was a little girl. I used to go out and look up at the stars and watch the clouds. I was filled with awe, and I wondered if I would ever know the One who made them.

I married at sixteen years of age, right after I finished high school. I had been planning to attend Brevard College to prepare and teach in the Methodist faith when I fell in love with a handsome young man. I proceeded to date him and persuaded my parents to give me permission to marry. When I was not quite seventeen I married George Parrish instead of attending college. One year later we had a baby boy, Darrell Parrish.

During this time, a Presbyterian girl who worked where I went to work knew Jesus. She had a relationship with the Lord I had never seen before. She didn't preach at me, but her life nagged me. I couldn't stand to be with her, and I couldn't stand to be away from her. I wanted to be near her so that what she had would rub off on me. But every time I got around her I felt convicted of my sin, though I did not understand then that conviction was what I was feeling.

She was praying for me, and the Methodist and Presbyterian people in her Bible class were praying for me. She knew I didn't know Jesus even though I was a Sunday school and VBS teacher, a member of the choir, and a faithful churchgoer. Surely I was going to heaven, but when I met this Presbyterian girl, by the law of contrast, I suddenly saw myself in a different light.

My Presbyterian friend didn't talk to me about my soul. She would just tell me about the good time they had had at the prayer meeting the night before and how precious Jesus was to her. She would talk about Jesus as if He were her sweetheart. It sounded strange to me. After all, wasn't God austere? Weren't we to be afraid of Him? Wasn't it irreverent to talk about Jesus as this girl did?

But she knew God in a way I had never known Him. I began to get so disturbed I couldn't sleep. I would awaken my husband and ask, "Honey, if I died before morning, would I go to heaven?"

He would always answer me, "That is the reason I married you, Fuchsia. You are a good girl. Yes, you would go to heaven."

That was all he knew, but someone else was telling me differently. The Third Person of the infinite Godhead became a companion in my room at night, trying to reveal Jesus to my darkened soul.

Old hymns that I had sung all my life in the Methodist church began echoing in the corridors of my spirit. I remember hearing the words, "And He walks with me, and He talks with me, and He tells me I am His own; and the joy we share as we tarry there none other has ever known. He speaks, and the sound of His voice is so sweet the birds hush their singing. . . . "[1]

As those words floated through my mind, I realized suddenly that either I was singing a lie or someone had written a fantasy. I did not know I was His own, and I had not heard Him talk to me. In those night hours the Holy Spirit began to address eternal values in my soul.

It Is Well With My Soul

A CITYWIDE REVIVAL was planned for my town, in

which all the churches participated. It seemed they did it more for the sake of unity than evangelism. They called on different preachers from the different denominations to preach, and they asked different people from various churches to sing.

At that time I could sing, but I didn't have the reality of a song in my heart. However, I was selected to be one of the singers for the revival, as was a friend of the Presbyterian girl who was fervently praying for my salvation. We were to sing a duet. Since I sang alto, I chose "It Is Well With My Soul" because it has a beautiful alto part. I suggested we sing that.

That night when we sang, I got through the first stanza of the song pretty well. By the second stanza my voice was faltering. During the third stanza tears were in my eyes, because for the first time in my life I realized it was *not* well with my soul. I wanted somebody to tell me what was wrong, to tell me that I could know Jesus. I needed to know *how* to make it well with my soul. People appreciated the performance of the song, but no one told me what I needed to know before I left the meeting that night.

When I got home I went to my bedroom and opened the dresser drawer to take out my nightgown. Suddenly I fell to my knees under a terrible power of conviction. Revelation of my need for a Savior had come to my heart.

The Holy Ghost came to my spirit and told me that I could know what I was singing was real. I cried out and said, "O God, if there is such a thing as *knowing* what I have been simply *singing* about in the church for years, tell me tonight. Let me know that I am ready to go to heaven. Let me know that I am a child of God."

In just a few moments, like a bolt of lightning, an old-fashioned Methodist salvation experience struck my inner man, and I was born again. I knew that I had been "translated . . . into the kingdom of his dear Son" (Col. 1:13). The melody of heaven became the anthem of my spirit. Sovereignly God had come to save this Methodist girl. He had heard the prayers of my Presbyterian friend and of those friends she had asked to pray for me.

That night I began to sing, and I have never stopped. I knew I had passed from death to life, and I wouldn't have given an angel in heaven a nickel to tell me I had been born again. I didn't know what to call it. I didn't know whether it was regeneration, conversion, being born again—I just knew it was real.

I jumped up off my knees and looked at my husband, who had been standing there witnessing what had happened, and I said, "Honey, I am all right with God. Something has happened to me. There is nothing between my soul and my Savior." I had moved out of darkness into light, and I knew that it was well with my soul.

I thought everyone in the world wanted to know it. I stopped everyone I saw at work to tell them about my experience. I testified to everyone I knew and to those I didn't know.

CALLED TO PREACH AND TEACH

SOMETIME LATER I had another sovereign visitation from God. I was in my room waiting for George to come home from work. As I lay in bed, I heard a voice louder than a normal tone of voice call my name. I raised up in the bed and answered questioningly, "Yes?" As I sat there for a moment, I sensed that my room was filled with the presence of God. No one answered my response so I lay back down.

A few moments later I was awakened, and I heard that voice call my name again. I decided it must be the people living upstairs in our house. I got up and looked up the stairwell, but I did not hear a sound. There was no one in the house. I went back and lay down on my bed. The third time I heard my name called aloud, I fell by my bedside trembling. I asked, "God, is this You?"

He said, "Yes, Fuchsia. I want you to preach and teach My Word."

One of the greatest blessings in my heritage is that my parents taught me to obey them. My daddy, the best friend I ever had on earth, taught me to obey even when I did not want to and to love to please him. So when the infinite, almighty, eternal, triune God—my heavenly Father—walked into my room, called me by my name, and told me He wanted me to preach and teach His Word, I didn't question whether I had an option to obey Him or not. My earthly daddy had taught me unconditional obedience.

I knew I had heard the voice of God, and no one could tell me I could not preach because I was a woman. I did not think that some committee or board needed to determine according to their theology whether I could or should feed His sheep as He had asked me to do.

I surrendered that night to God, although I didn't know how or when or where I would fulfill the mandate He placed on my life. I was a wife and young mother. It did not seem likely that I could get the preparation I would need to preach the gospel. But God always provides where He has commanded an obedient heart.

My husband was a petty officer in the Navy during the latter part of the Korean War. He was called to active duty, and I was able to enter Bible college as God sovereignly opened the door. God sat me down in Bible school at John Wesley College in Greensboro, North Carolina, while my husband was away in the military and my boy was little.

After graduation God led me out into the ministry, opening doors for me to preach the Word. I had never heard of a woman preacher. My mother was so distressed at the prospect of my preaching that she wore black and cried and felt as though her daughter were dead. But I knew I had heard from God, and I could not be deterred. (In later years, happily, I became my mother and father's pastor. They became two of my greatest supporters.)

God had sovereignly revealed Himself to me as Savior and Lord and had called me into the ministry. He opened the way for me to attend Martinsville Bible College, Aldergate University, and to do graduate work at the University of North Carolina. I knew I was called to preach His Word, though that was more unusual for a woman in that time than it is now. Yet He opened doors across the country for meetings.

My first husband, George, was saved in our home one week after he witnessed my dramatic conversion experience. He became a wonderful soloist and sang in our meetings. Later, when we pastored, he led the music and directed the choir as well. We worked in the kingdom as a team, walking happily together in ministry. We were sincere believers, living according to the understanding we had from our training in the Word. But God put us on a painful path that brought us to a place of revelation we never knew existed.

SURROUNDED BY TRAGEDY

MY FAMILY HAD not escaped tragedy. My parents had suffered the loss of two sons in childhood, Morton and Melvin, to a genetic disease. Then, not long after I started pastoring, Everette, my only brother still living, came to our church with his son. He told me that his son was showing some alarming symptoms that indicated the onset of the illness that had manifested itself in Hodgkins. For months we watched the child slowly die. By now all the boys in my family were gone except my own son and my one remaining brother. Everette was left with only his lovely daughter, Sylvia Turner Dagenhart.

Then my daddy became ill. I watched this great man, a member of my church board who had walked with God and was so devout—my "papa"— waste away. All we could do was stand helplessly by, not knowing why these things had to be.

Then one day, during the last stages of my daddy's illness, my body too began to register frightening signs of illness. I felt instinctively that my days of ministry would soon be over. I returned home to spend some time with my daddy before his death. We had a most providential conversation during one day of my visit. I had been my daddy's pastor for nine years, and we enjoyed sharing from the Word together. But that day he walked into the room where I sat, his face showing great pain and with his Bible in his hand.

He looked at me and said, "Daughter, I think we have missed something, haven't we?"

"Why, Daddy?" I questioned.

"I keep reading about Elijah. Elijah knew a God I don't think we know in our day." He looked me straight in the face and shot out his question, "Pastor, where is the God of Elijah?"

I carefully explained to him what I had been taught concerning healing and miracles. I said gently, "Daddy, we don't need that now. The Scriptures teach that when that which is perfect is come, these gifts will be done away with. Jesus is that perfect One who has come, so we don't need miracles and healing anymore. We have the written Word; the Word has come." That was the last cogent conversation I ever had with my daddy.

I had gone home to help my mother take care of Daddy. But I began to hurt so intensely that I said regretfully to my sister-in-law, "Don't tell my mother why, but I am not going to be able to stay through the weekend. I am suffering so badly that I must go home to see my doctor. Please don't tell Mother. She has enough with Daddy." Without explaining why, I told Mother I was going home.

Saturday morning I went to my study with every bone of my body feeling as if it were breaking, especially in my spine. When I got into my study, a pain hit the base of my neck, went down my spine, shot into both of my legs, and seemed to jerk my backbone. I fell to the floor and cried in pain. Then I struggled to my feet and went out the door screaming for help. I didn't know where I was.

My husband and friends found me, picked me up, and carried me to my bed. I was not aware of my surroundings until the following Tuesday. As I lay there, I became aware of my husband sitting at the foot of my bed. He was talking to a Nazarene preacher.

I heard him ask, "Why? Can you tell me why this woman, who loves God with all her heart and has studied His Word all her life to be able to train men and women in the gospel message, has to suffer this?"

My first thought was that I didn't want him to become bitter. I said, "Honey, it is all right. Don't worry."

They wheeled me into a hospital in North Carolina, where my testimony is documented in their files. They packed me in sandbags and devices to sustain my body. They gave me cortisone and other kinds of medication to relieve my pain. Prior to my admittance, I had written out my funeral arrangements and picked out my pallbearers. My tombstone was erected in the Overlook Cemetery in Eden, North Carolina. The only things missing were a date of death on the tombstone and a body in the lot.

One afternoon shortly after my husband left my hospital room, I heard him coming back down the hall. He had been gone only a few minutes, and I knew it wasn't time for him to return. Yet I recognized his step coming toward my room. As he approached the door to my room he said, "Honey?"

I said, "Yes, dear, come in." My head was packed as it lay on the pillow, and I was lying between sandbags. I said, "You are back soon. Come over where I can see you."

As soon as he came into the room, I knew something was wrong. I saw that someone was behind him. The nurse put a shot in my arm, a precautionary measure the doctor was taking. He had said to my husband, "It will be hard for her to bear this news." He knew that my daddy was one of the dearest people on earth to me.

George said, "Honey, I bring you bad news. Papa is dead. He left today." I began to weep.

In spite of my physical condition, I determined to go to my daddy's funeral. The nurses packed a stretcher carefully to make sure it would not hurt me. They carried me to an ambulance and drove the sixty miles to my parents' home. I rode to the funeral in an ambulance.

It was the sixth time I had heard a preacher say "ashes to ashes and dust to dust" when burying a precious member of my family. I didn't ever want to hear those words again. I asked them not to lower my daddy into the grave in my presence. They placed him on the mound of dirt covered with green turf, flanked with a large array of lovely flowers—the expression of love and sympathy from our friends.

As the coach turned around, I looked out the back window and said, "Good-bye, Papa. I will be with you in a few months." I felt that I would be with him soon. I was ready to meet God. I was "paid up, prayed up, packed up, and ready to go up." I had preached seventeen years for Him, pastoring and teaching. I had carried the gospel to many people; I had taught Bible school students; I had preached in camp meetings. I knew I was ready to go to heaven. I felt my ministry was over.

I was transferred to Charlotte, North Carolina, to

the care of another bone specialist. One day, several weeks after my daddy's funeral, the doctor walked into my hospital room and said, "Fuchsia, we are going to fasten you into a brace and let you go home for a few weeks now. Then we will bring you in and fuse your back together to keep you from hemorrhaging." The nurses fitted me with the brace, and I went home.

A MIRACULOUS INTERVENTION

I HAD BEEN home a few days when I received word that a teachers' meeting for many of the friends with whom I had taught was scheduled on the following Sunday morning. I had a friend call the doctor to ask if I could be carried to that service. The doctor said it wouldn't matter either way, just to be prepared. I took medicine for the pain, and my friend drove me sixty miles to the church, not knowing if it would be my last service.

The church where the meeting was to be held was not one I would have chosen to attend. It was the First Pentecostal Holiness Church of Danville, Virginia. I was going only because the teachers with whom I had worked were going to be there that morning. It was one of those churches I considered strange. Over six hundred people attended the Pentecostal church the morning I went.

As a college professor, I had been teaching and pastoring as well as doing radio work. I considered myself to be intelligent. And I loved God with all my heart. I believed in commitment, consecration, and holiness. Yet, as a result of my choice to attend a strange service, I was carried to a church with which I did not agree doctrinally or experientially in their Pentecostal experiences.

Later I learned that at four o'clock on that Sunday morning God had awakened the seventy-year-old retired superintendent of the Pentecostal Holiness Church, Brother Dale, who was to be the guest speaker that morning in the church he had formerly pastored, and told him to preach a certain message. God had arranged to move the current pastor of the church out of the pulpit that morning. (I told the pastor later that if he had been preaching that morning, I would be dead. Everything was done "in order" and according to the clock. He dismissed his congregation at noon sharp.)

Though the church had lost some of its former revival spirit, a prayer group of about seventy-five godly people met every Monday night in the basement of the church to ask God for revival. In that prayer group was one of my former students, who was also one of those teachers with whom I was meeting that morning.

She had been asking the group to pray for my healing. She called my next-door neighbor, a Lutheran woman, every week to see how I was doing. Every week my neighbor would tell her, "She is worse." And Edna would respond, "Praise the Lord." My Lutheran neighbor thought Edna was strange.

When I was carried into the church that Sunday morning, the prayer group was ecstatic because they knew that the stage had been set for God to do a miracle.

I had said to my friend who drove me to the church, "If nothing else is accomplished this morning,

I want you to bring Edna to me. Before I leave this world, I would like to get her straightened out. She has gotten into that strange church and is mixed up. I really want to get Edna straightened out." I did not know that it was not Edna—but me—who was to be straightened out that day.

During the service, the guest speaker preached the message God had awakened him to tell him to preach. He had reasoned with God, telling Him that he had already preached that sermon to this church when he pastored it. He said that God simply said to him, "You preach; I keep the records."

He began his sermon with deep conviction and fervency, declaring to us the reality of the God of Elijah. My thoughts raced back to my last conversation with my daddy. I found myself gripped by this godly preacher's words. Suddenly he moved from behind the pulpit, stood in front of me on the platform, and looked me straight in the eye. He said, "My beloved, you may have followed behind the dearest one on earth to you and left him on a green mound. But he didn't take his God away from you. He wants you to know that the God of Elijah is in this church today, and He is the same today as He has always been." I felt my daddy had gotten to heaven and told God he had a dumb daughter down on earth who needed to know the God of Elijah is alive today. He then asked God, "Please straighten her out."

As he brought his message on "If We Had the Faith of Elijah, We Could See What Elijah Saw," I was stunned. Then I felt someone punch me in the ribs. I knew who it was because I had been talking to Him for seventeen years. He was my Savior. He told me to go forward for prayer. I debated because they were not giving an altar call. The preacher started to close the service, but then he paused to say, "I feel strangely led to sing an old Methodist hymn. Do you know that old Methodist hymn, 'Majestic Sweetness Sits Enthroned'?"

The song leader replied, "Yes, we do. Let's take out our songbooks." So the congregation of the First Pentecostal Holiness Church sang a Methodist hymn to this Methodist pastor who was sitting there in pain with her funeral arrangements already made.

Again I felt the Holy Spirit say, "Go forward for prayer."

Again I responded, "There is no altar call. How am I going to get up there?" The church continued with the last stanza, "He saw me plunged in deep distress and flew to my relief."

Again I heard Him say, "Go forward for prayer."

About that time they were ready to finish the song, and I prayed, "God, if this is You, make them sing another stanza."

They finished the song and closed their books. But the speaker got up and said, "Isn't there another stanza to that song?"

"Yes, there is," the song leader replied.

"Could we sing it, please?" the speaker asked. So they sang it.

I pulled on the girl's dress who had taken me to the church and said, "Stand me up." She looked at me strangely, but she heard my tone and knew she dared not fail to respond. So she stood me up. Dragging my weakened body in my braces, I picked up my Bible, went up to the little man, looked into his face, and said, "Sir, I don't know why I am here. But I have a feeling that God would like these people to pray for me."

He said, "All right." He reached into the pulpit and got a small bottle out. Then he "greased me" and prayed so gently, "In the name of Jesus," like I had never heard it said before. It changed my life—and my theology—totally. Suddenly my eyes were on Jesus, and I had a foretaste of the glory that is yet to be revealed in the church when Jesus stands in our midst.

Nothing dramatic happened in my body when he prayed. God simply spoke to me about my consecration. He asked me to surrender to Him the same way I had the night He had called me to preach. I did. In my limited understanding, I did not know but that I had perhaps just been anointed for my burial. Dragging myself in my braces, I started to return to my seat.

When I reached my chair at the seventh pew, suddenly I had my first vision of the spiritual world. I heard a voice thunder, "If ye be willing and obedient, ye shall eat the good of the land" (Isa. 1:19). I thought everyone heard it. In an instant, the words "of the land" stood up like red neon lights before my eyes. Those words were the first thing I ever saw like that in the spirit.

I stood as if frozen and watched those words, in huge red letters at the back of the sanctuary, and realized at that moment that they didn't refer to heaven. Eating the good of the land meant right here and now. I grabbed that understanding by faith. And I had a witness in the spirit that I was going to live, though I didn't yet know that I was going to be healed.

Then I heard the Lord ask me, "Are you willing to be identified with these people—to be one of them?"

Before I had time to bring my theology to argue against Him, I said, "Yes, Lord, I will be identified with these people." Then I turned and looked at the man who had preached that morning and said, "Sir, may I say something?"

He said, "Of course. Testimonies are always in order in this church."

"I am going to live. Jesus just told me so." I held my Bible and stood there in tears, still in my braces, thinking that that was how I would have to preach the gospel.

I turned again and started to my seat. Suddenly the power of God struck the base of my neck and coursed through my body. The miraculous, healing power of God put me back together instantly. It was the infinite, triune, omnipotent God who touched me that morning. I was made every whit whole inside my organs, my blood condition, and my bones. And when He turned me loose, I ran and danced and shouted. I had been struck by resurrection power, which healed me and set me free.

Two hours later—same service, same people—over three hundred of the six hundred people present had been visited by the Holy Spirit. God had brought revival in answer to the prayers of those who had prayed every Monday night for almost a year for revival and for my healing.

That morning I ran the aisles when I didn't believe in it. I had my hands up, though I had never raised them in praise before. I shouted, and the other people shouted. I finally ended up in the corner. They said I danced and shouted, "I don't hurt!" Then

I started to take off my braces. Previously, I had suffered worse pain than I thought possible for a human being to suffer.

Finally, about one hour and twenty minutes later, I was standing in the corner of the church with my hands up, having exhausted my vocabulary trying to express my gratitude for this unexpected miracle. I heard myself saying, "Bless the Lord, O my soul, and all that is within me, bless His holy name." As I was standing there facing the wall, tears of joy rolling down my cheeks, trying to thank Him, my soul began to bless Him in a language that I had never learned or heard before. Not only was I healed from the top of my head to the tip of my toes, but I was filled with the Holy Ghost.

I drove my own automobile sixty miles home that day. On the way I stopped at my mother's house. I went running in to tell her the good news, and she almost fainted when she saw me. The following Tuesday I went to see my doctor. As I walked into the office unassisted and without braces, I told the nurse not to say a word to the doctor. I jumped up backwards onto the examining table and sat there smiling. The nurse was dismayed at my actions and cried out for me to be careful. She left the room to call the doctor.

He was a Baptist lay preacher. When he had examined me thoroughly and taken x-rays and done blood work, he looked at me and said, "Fuchsia, this is a miracle. Jump down from there, girl."

I jumped down, and he put his arm around my waist. We walked out into the reception area to a room full of people, and the doctor said to the receptionist, "Strike her name out of our book. She has been on a doctor's book since she was eighteen years old. The only thing she will need now is some vitamins, because I have a feeling she is not going to stop wherever she goes."

Then he turned to the people in the waiting room and said, "This is what faith will do." He pronounced me completely healed.

MORE WONDERFUL THAN HEALING

I KNEW THAT I would not have lived more than a few months if God had not miraculously intervened in my life and healed my body. That was more than thirty years ago, and I have enjoyed the results of that miracle all these years. Yet, something more wonderful than physical healing happened to me that Sunday morning. Within a few days of my healing, I realized that the baptism of the Holy Spirit I had received that day had ushered me into a new relationship with God.

My divine "Teacher" had come to fill me with Himself and to split open the veil between my soul and my spirit. He intervened in my desperate circumstances and healed me miraculously when my mind did not believe the doctrine of healing. For the first time in my life I began to understand, through revelation, the same Scriptures I had studied and taught faithfully for many years. They came alive to me, not as information, but as power that was working in me and transforming my life. ❧

Four

My "Teacher" Moved In

DURING THE YEARS that followed my healing and baptism in the Holy Spirit, I was thrust into a new relationship with God. I experienced supernatural revelation and a walk in the power of the Holy Spirit that I never dreamed possible. Apart from my salvation experience and the supernatural calling of God to the ministry, I had not experienced visions or other divine visitations. That all changed when the Holy Spirit moved in to become my Teacher.

Though I had heard God call me by my name to preach and teach His Word and had seen Him open doors for me and prepare the way for seventeen years of ministry, I now began to receive revelation from my Teacher—the blessed Holy Spirit—who had come to teach me the Word the way He wrote it.

THE HOLY SPIRIT'S CLASSROOM

I FELT THAT the reason God had to reveal Himself to me the way He did is because I was so dumb. I didn't know anything about walking in the Spirit, though I thought I did. I was taught holiness in the Methodist church. But after my healing and baptism in the Spirit, I moved into a life of divine revelation that I had not known anything about. All of a sudden, I was healed when I didn't believe in it and speaking in tongues when I had taught against it.

The day after I received the baptism of the Holy Spirit, I took a small footstool and sat down as if I were sitting at Jesus' feet. I said these words to my Teacher, the Holy Spirit: "Now, healing has happened to me, and I was taught it was not for today. And I have experienced the baptism of the Holy Spirit in a way that I did not believe in. How do I know that the rest of what I have been taught is right? So let's start over."

The Holy Spirit spoke to me in that moment: "You run your seminary classes based on sixty- or ninety-minute sessions. I don't. I live here in your spirit. I have moved in to be your Teacher, and my classroom is never closed. I wrote the Book. You may come in anytime you want and ask any question you want." Then He so sweetly added, "And I will never scold you for asking."

Incredulously, I ventured, "I can ask anything I want to ask, and You will teach me the Book?" He said, "Yes."

"All right," I replied, "teach me what is in the Book." I had spent seventeen years studying, and I don't despise what I have studied. That knowledge of the Word brought me to the point that I could receive true revelation of it.

After the first session of revelation, for the first four months after my healing I did not hear from God at all. There was no life in the Scriptures when I read them, except for a few verses that my Teacher gave me. Otherwise, my Book was a closed Book. Nothing spoke to me. One of the verses that did speak to me was: "For the vision is yet for an appointed time, but at the end it shall speak, and not lie: though it tarry, wait for it; because it will surely come, it will not tarry" (Hab. 2:3).

Another verse He gave me was: "Trust in the LORD with all thine heart; and lean not unto thine own understanding" (Prov. 3:5). And the one following, "In all thy ways acknowledge him, and he shall direct thy paths" (Prov. 3:6). These were the only living words that guided me during those weeks. During that time I received invitations to share my healing testimony, but otherwise I was not invited to preach anywhere.

But finally, after the silence of those four months, my Teacher began my instruction. For the next five years I slept very little—two or three nights a week perhaps. On the other evenings I would study the Word, losing all track of time.

As the Holy Spirit would quicken a truth to me, whole books of the Bible would open and relate to each other in my mind. I saw how the Book of Leviticus related to Hebrews, Joshua to Ephesians, and I walked the floor, shaking my head and staggering in my ability to grasp it all.

One night the Spirit spoke to me, saying, "Abraham staggered not."

I replied, "Please don't stop teaching me." On those nights of marathon study, just before dawn I would lie down for a few hours of rest, filled with awe at what I had learned.

THE GLORY CLOUD

THE DAY AFTER I was healed, I was at home trying to comprehend what had happened to me. I knew I was healed. But what about those tongues? In that moment, the Lord told me to read the fifty-third chapter of Isaiah. I read it, and for the first time I saw that healing was a part of the atonement act of Jesus. Isaiah declared:

> But he was wounded for our transgressions, he was bruised for our iniquities: the chastisement of our peace was upon him; and with his stripes we are healed.
>
> —ISAIAH 53:5

After reading His wonderful truth, I went into my kitchen and began to mop the floor. I was so glad I could do that again. I was praising the Lord because I wouldn't have to have people clean my house anymore. All of a sudden, as I mopped my floor, a cloud appeared over me. It was clearly a cloud—not a shadow—and I saw it with my natural eyes.

My first thought was, *That must be the glory cloud.* Then I corrected myself, *No, the glory cloud was over the temple.* I looked at it and continued to thank the Lord.

From the thirteeth day of April until I returned from Atlanta in September, that visible cloud went with me everywhere. If I went to the grocery store, it rode over my basket. If I drove my automobile, it was over my windshield. When I went to bed at night, it stood over my bed. If I got up and went to the bathroom, it went with me. The presence of God was in that cloud. My husband, George, was aware that it was in the house, though he could not see it.

Sometime in August I was baking biscuits and cooking supper while my husband was mowing the yard. He knocked on the door because he had grass on his feet and said, "Honey, someone here wants to see you. He is a minister."

No minister had visited me since April. We had recently moved to this town, and we didn't have any Pentecostal friends. I felt like a woman without a country. I took off my apron and went to the door to greet the minister.

"Hello, sir," I greeted him warmly.

"Hello," he responded. "I am Dr. Kerr from the First Pentecostal Holiness Church. I understand you are a Methodist minister and have received the baptism of the Holy Spirit."

I said, "Yes, sir."

We invited him to come in, and after we visited for a few minutes he asked me curiously, "Did I interrupt you? Were you praying?"

"No, sir," I said. "I was cooking supper."

As though somewhat in awe he responded by saying, "This place is full of God's presence."

Tears began to roll down my face, and I said, "Do you see that cloud?"

"No, but I don't doubt that there is one here," he answered.

"Sir, you may think I am crazy, but there is a cloud in this room, and it has been here for several months."

My husband spoke up and said, "It has been here since the day after she was healed. This house has had the presence of God in it from April until now."

"I don't know what is in that cloud, sir," I said to the minister. "It keeps getting heavier and blacker. But I know that when it bursts I am going to be under it. And I believe the direction for my future is in that cloud."

PENTECOSTAL CONNECTIONS

LATER I WENT TO a Pentecostal camp meeting with a friend shortly after I was healed. It was big news that a Methodist minister had received the baptism of the Spirit. (This was at the beginning of the Charismatic renewal during which many denominational people received the baptism of the Holy Spirit.) As a Spirit-filled Methodist professor, I was a novelty.

The Assembly of God camp meeting director came to me in the lunch line and asked me to give my testimony that night in the service. Because I was so new to this experience, I did not want to expose my ignorance by testifying in front of Pentecostal people. I didn't even know their terminology. The director asked me to take about ten minutes to share what God had done for me. The girl who had taken me to the camp meeting saw my hesitancy and asked me, "Won't you?"

I answered her, "Well, if I am still here tonight I will."

I tried to go home that day, but my friend

wouldn't let me. She said, "No, you are going to testify." So I stayed.

Rev. Ralph Byrd, known fondly as "Daddy" Byrd, was there as the speaker for the camp meeting. At that time he pastored a great church in Atlanta, Georgia, that raised up missionaries and leaders and sent them around the world. The weather had been inclement, and it seemed that it affected Reverend Byrd's throat. He was not anxious to attempt to preach that evening.

The president of the camp introduced me as the Methodist minister who had recently received the baptism of the Holy Spirit and asked me to come forward and share my testimony. I stood up and gave my testimony of how God had healed me from a deathbed and filled me with the Holy Spirit. I concluded my testimony by saying, "I may be a woman without a country, but I am not a sheep without a shepherd."

That statement expressed my inner perplexity. I didn't know where to go. I had been called back to the Methodist college to be the pastor. Before my new experiences in God I would have given anything to hold that position. But when I went to the college and preached, I knew it was not the place for me.

So I went home from the camp meeting, still needing direction for my life yet hearing Him say, "You may not go now." But the presence of the Lord still hovered over me in the form of a cloud.

PROVIDENTIAL INVITATION

NOT LONG AFTER the camp meeting, I was visiting in my son Darrell's home when I received a long distance phone call. As I walked to the phone, the Lord spoke to me and said, "You may go now."

I said, "Hello," and found that I was speaking to Rev. Ralph Byrd, the speaker for the camp meeting.

He said, "I heard you give your testimony at the camp meeting, and I would like you to come to my church in Atlanta to preach in some special services."

I responded, "Sir, you don't know me. I can't preach Pentecostal. I don't know how."

"We will trust God for that," he said firmly.

"How long do you want me to stay?"

"We will trust God for that also. I only know that God has not released me from your testimony since that night."

I wasn't used to hearing ministers talk like that. "All right, I will come," I acquiesced hesitantly. The cloud went with me all the way to Atlanta. I was a foreigner in that church. They were flowing in worship and praise such as I had never experienced. After I had been there a week, I walked into Daddy Byrd's office on Friday afternoon to tell him that I was going home.

Before I said anything, he greeted me with, "I had just sent for you. I want you to call your husband and tell him you are not coming home this week."

I said, "I beg your pardon?"

He continued earnestly, "You are not through here. I will talk to your husband if you like."

"Dr. Byrd, I can't preach Pentecostal," I argued. "I feel like a foreigner here."

"Leave that to me," he replied. "I want you to give your complete testimony on Sunday night." He had asked me to wait until he could advertise that service.

So on the following Sunday night I gave my testimony. The church was full. People had come to hear how a Methodist preacher was healed and filled with the Holy Spirit.

A VISION OF MY DADDY

SOMEONE IN MY FAMILY, who then did not understand the Pentecostal experience, had told me, "If your daddy knew what you've become, he would turn over in his grave."

That comment was very hurtful to me because I loved my daddy so much. My family thought it was wonderful that I was healed, but it was not acceptable to them to be a part of "those Pentecostal" people.

But a wonderful thing happened to me as I stood in the church that night. Standing on the platform of that church, I had a vision. As I stood there, I saw four men walk into the church. They stood in the doorway and viewed the congregation. One of them looked straight at me. I was surprised to see that it was my daddy.

Instinctively I knew that I was seeing him in his glorified body. He could see me, and I could see him. As our eyes met, I ran my hands up and down my sides and said to him, "Look at me, Papa; I am healed."

Then I pointed to the congregation and said, "Look at these people." He looked around at the people and smiled his biggest smile. Then he disappeared. In that instant I knew that my daddy was very happy for me. And I declared, "Devil, you are a liar. My daddy is happy for me."

I realized then that when my daddy had arrived in heaven he asked God to please send the truth to his dumb daughter down on earth.

A CLOUDBURST

AFTER I GAVE my testimony that night, people poured down to the altar. I was so excited at their response that when I went to my room I began to praise and thank the Lord for what He had done. The cloud that had hovered over me for several months was right over my bed. As the weeks had passed, it had gotten heavier and heavier, like a cloud that is about to burst with rain.

After I had gone to bed, the cloud engulfed me and began to burst. It gushed out floods, and I started laughing. I was experiencing Holy Ghost laughter, rejoicing, and joy that I could not contain. Because I was a guest in a home and did not want to disturb my hosts, I picked up a pillow, stuck it over my mouth, and buried my face in it to muffle the sound. I laughed and rejoiced and could not stop. Waves of joy and laughter flooded over me. For almost two hours I tried to keep it contained so I would not wake my hosts.

Then I heard a knock on my door. The lady of the house asked if she could come in. When she saw me with my mouth buried in a pillow, laughing, she said, "God is in this house! I have been in every room of this house looking for the presence of God. I went into the bathroom, the kitchen, and living room—He is not there. So I decided He must be in here. Can I come in?"

Convulsed in laughter, I said, "Please, come in."

I was not aware of what happened from that time until four o'clock the next afternoon. The Holy Spirit kept flowing through me in waves of joy and rejoicing. I suppose it was the kind of "drunken" experience that people are enjoying again in this latest move of God.

My hostess enjoyed it with me. It was an awesome, God-conscious time for the remainder of that day. Late that afternoon she finally exclaimed, "We need to think about getting you ready to go to church. You have to preach tonight."

I asked dubiously, "What am I going to preach?" I didn't have a sermon prepared. She had to help me dress because of my "drunken" state. The cloud had burst, and the presence of God was flooding my soul.

When I got to church, Brother Byrd took one look at me and said to his associate, "I knew I was supposed to bring her here."

As I stood to preach, I began by reading the thirty-fifth chapter of Isaiah. As I read I started crying uncontrollably.

> The desert and the parched land will be glad;
> the wilderness will rejoice and blossom. Like
> the crocus, it will burst into bloom; it will
> rejoice greatly and shout for joy. The glory of
> Lebanon will be given to it, the splendor of
> Carmel and Sharon; they will see the glory of
> the LORD, the splendor of our God.
>
> —ISAIAH 35:1–2, NIV

I had preached from this passage before with a historical perspective, but now I was seeing the reality of it. I had experienced the rejoicing and joy

45

of seeing the glory of God upon my life. I stood there and preached what I had never seen before. Then I started weeping and couldn't speak anymore. The altar began to fill with people. Daddy Byrd said to someone nearby, "She is going to be all right. God has her now."

He asked God to let me stay there to minister to his church. Though I went home often for several days at a time to be with my husband, I ministered in Atlanta for most of the next three months. Pastor Byrd was a faithful mentor to me, giving me sound guidance and answering many of my questions. It was there that I experienced so many glorious hours with my Teacher—the Holy Spirit.

A GUERNSEY COW?

BROTHER BYRD MET with me every Monday morning after I had ministered in churches in the area. As he and his wife sat at breakfast with me, we shared what God was doing, and I would ask him questions about things I did not understand. Then I would share with them what God was showing me in the Word, and he listened intently, reveling in my excitement.

One day as we were sharing he looked at me and said with a grin, "You remind me of a Guernsey cow."

Startled by such a comparison, I replied, "I beg your pardon?"

He continued, "You are so full of the milk of the Word that you are bursting with it and looking for every calf around that you can feed. You are like the Guernsey cow that has milk enough for many calves. You are going to feed your 'little sisters.'" (See Song of Solomon 8:10, NIV.)

When I declared in that August camp meeting, "I may be a woman without a country, but I am not a sheep without a shepherd," I did not dream how my Shepherd would lead me to a church of people who cared for me and would help me to walk into my future as it burst upon me from the glory cloud that hovered over me.

Through many precious visitations of God, the Holy Spirit unlocked the Book that I had so loved and given my life to study. Those first years of revelation of the Word to my heart have formed the basis of my teaching today. They were foundational to the fresh revelation that is ever unfolding more clearly as we continue to walk with Him. ⌒

Five

Revelation of Worship

I T WAS IN the church in Atlanta that I first saw
people truly worship. I had never heard people
talk to the Lord in love language, saying things like,
"I love You, Lord." I was fascinated by their expressions of worship. Each night after I preached, I
turned the service over to the pastor, who gave the
altar call. I told him that I didn't know how to close
this kind of meeting. He would just say to the congregation, "Let's come and love Jesus before we go
home." And I was amazed that everyone would
come to the altar.

During one of the services, while people were
singing praises at the beginning of the service, I
looked down from the platform where I was seated
and saw a pretty little red-headed woman worshiping God. She was perhaps thirty-five years of

age, and she was loving Jesus. Her face looked as if it were lit by a thousand-watt bulb. Tears were flowing down her cheeks, and I heard her saying, "I love You, Jesus."

As I watched her, it seemed her face got brighter and brighter. I couldn't hear what she was saying from where I was, and I was curious. So I walked down off the platform and stood in front of her. She ignored me. I leaned over and said, "You and the Lord are having a good time, aren't you, honey?" Still she didn't pay attention to me. I was insulted. I thought, *Doesn't she know I am the guest evangelist?*

As I stood near her I heard her say, "You are the lily of the valley. I love You. You are the bright and morning star." I recognized that she was quoting love phrases from the Song of Solomon. She continued, "Thank You for being my husband, my lover." Somewhat awed, I turned and went back to the platform to sit down.

But I could not take my eyes off her. I knew she was experiencing something that I never had. I watched her awhile, then walked back down to stand by her. She was still lost in worship, though I did not understand that then. So I returned to the platform a second time. Still watching her, I thought, *Maybe she doesn't hear well.*

So I walked down a third time and stood behind her so I could speak directly into her ear. Again I said to her, "You and the Lord are having a good time together, aren't you?" What I really wanted to say was, "What is going on? I don't understand what it is that I am seeing you enjoy." I thought she could explain it to me, but she still did not acknowledge my presence.

This time when I returned to the platform I felt someone punch me. I recognized that it was the Lord trying to get my attention, as He had done before. He spoke to me then so sweetly, "Fuchsia, you can have that if you want it." I didn't even know what *that* was.

I went to my room after the service and got on my knees. I said to the Lord, "All right, what is it? You said I could have the thing that made that girl so 'lost' she didn't know I was there. What is *that?*"

The Lord answered me, "I seek a people who worship Me in spirit and truth."

I asked, "Is that worship? Then what have I been doing all these years?"

He was so kind. He didn't scold me. "Without this revelation of worship," He replied gently, "you have simply been having religious services."

"How can I have that?" I cried out. "Teach me to worship."

Then the Lord asked me three simple questions. First He inquired, "What would you do if you had just heard the gates of heaven click behind your heels, and you knew you were through with the devil forever?"

I responded vehemently, "You know I hate him!" I had spent months in a hospital as a patient, and I had followed behind casket after casket of family members who were being buried. I continued, "I would shout 'Glory!'"

He said, "Shout it." And I did.

I told Him that I would cry, "Hallelujah!"

He said, "Do it." And I did.

Then He asked me what I would do if I looked up and saw Jesus for the first time.

I said that I would bow at His feet, kiss His nail-scarred hands, and wash His feet with my tears.

He said, "Do it."

I meditated on the efficacious, vicarious, substitutionary, and mediatorial work of Calvary, and suddenly I had a fresh glimpse of the Lamb of God. I began to bow before the Lamb who was slain, but He asked me to look up into His face. "When you see Me face to face," He asked, "what will you tell Me?"

When I heard those words, it was as if a dam within my soul broke; torrents of praise flooded my lips. I told Him He was wonderful, and I recited the attributes of God I had learned in Bible college. I told Him He was omnipotent, omniscient, omnipresent, immutable, immaculate, emancipated, incarnate, and divine. When I finished, He asked me if these were the only adjectives I had for Him.

With a sense of awe I responded simply, "You are wonderful."

A picture came to my mind, and I saw the face of Jesus before me as if it were framed. Then the frame faded. As I looked into His face, I told Him how much I loved Him. I had never done that in my life. I told Him how precious He was to me. I went on and on, trying to express my love for Him with my limited vocabulary.

While I was answering His three questions, it seemed as if just a few moments of time had passed. But it had actually been an hour and a half. For the first time in my life I had been in the presence of God in such a way that I had lost all consciousness of time. I had finally experienced true worship pouring out of my soul as I expressed my love and adoration for God. All my years of

Bible training, study, and ministry had not brought me to the place of worship that a few moments of divine revelation in His presence had done.

Since that time I have experienced the revelation of His presence through my praise and worship many times. And I have also learned to experience the glory of His presence as it is revealed through His precious Word.

Of course, the biblical pattern of worship is based on the surrender of the heart to the lordship of Christ. We see this in Genesis, the Book of Beginnings. When God asked Abraham to offer up his only son, Isaac, he told those traveling with him, "Abide ye here with the ass; and I and the lad will go yonder and worship, and come again to you" (Gen. 22:5). Without that heart reality demonstrated by Abraham in complete obedience and submission to the will of God, we will never experience true worship in spirit and truth, no matter what musical expression or other kind of "expression" we offer Him.

Having that heart attitude, we are ready to receive a revelation of our Lord that will evoke true worship and adoration from our souls. That is the difference between religious expressions and true worship. I am so grateful that the Holy Spirit taught me to worship God in spirit and in truth.

THE HALLELUJAH CHORUS

As I BEGAN to find my "home" among Pentecostal people, there was one word I heard them use over and over in worship. That word was *hallelujah*. I remembered how I had visited old-time camp meetings where occasionally some little grandma waved her handkerchief and shouted *hallelujah!* But people didn't praise God audibly in the Methodist churches that I was accustomed to. When I got into Pentecost, I thought the people were noisy. It seemed their favorite expression was *hallelujah.*

That word rang in my spirit, and I joined them in shouting *hallelujah* as my highest expression of wonder and awe in the presence of God. I usually don't say anything else other than *hallelujah*—my spirit responds to the power of God with that one word. Later I learned that *hallelujah* is the highest word of praise we can use.

As part of my ministry in the Methodist church, I had led choirs in wonderful musical presentations of Handel's "Hallelujah Chorus." I wondered why Spirit-filled Pentecostals did not sing it and what they would sound like if they did. *They would understand the reality of what they were singing,* I thought. The symphony orchestra approached Handel's *Messiah* as classical music literature, but they could not interpret the reality of the message like those who understood whom they were worshiping. But to my disappointment, it seemed Pentecostals were not interested in such music.

I visited Pentecostal churches with big choirs, but no one ever sang the "Hallelujah Chorus." For months I kept telling the Lord I wanted to hear the "Hallelujah Chorus."

One night at home, after my husband and I had been asleep for several hours, at about two o'clock in the morning, I heard a sound that woke me up. It was glorious! As I lay there awake, listening, I recognized the "Hallelujah Chorus" from Handel's *Messiah.* I got out of bed and went to sit down in my living room chair where I enjoyed the "Hallelujah Chorus" in its entirety.

There was not a soul in the house playing music. My husband was the only other person in the house, and he was asleep. There were no stereos playing, no cassette tapes, no CDs. There was no one driving by with music playing in their car. I sat alone and listened to a fantastic performance of the "Hallelujah Chorus." I felt as if I were going to explode. It seemed I heard it like I had never heard it in my life.

When the choir sang the glorious last *Hal-le-lu-jah,* the Holy Spirit asked me, "Is that what you wanted to hear?" I sat there breathless, wondering how to explain what I had just experienced.

Don't ask me where it came from. I don't know. I don't know who sang it. But if I died and went to heaven right now, I would still declare that I heard the "Hallelujah Chorus." It was a heavenly sound. That hallelujah praise was released in my spirit, and it was not long after that experience that I began to teach worship. To this day, when I hear a choir sing the "Hallelujah Chorus," my spirit leaps, and I feel helpless in trying to find an expression for my joy. I believe I heard the heavens sing it that night to me.

A VISION OF JESUS

IT WAS EARLY in my days in Atlanta that I had a vision of Jesus. I was staying in the home of the Jacksons, and we had just returned from a service on Saturday night. My hosts had gone to bed, and I knelt to pray in their den before I went to bed. I felt such a solemnity of God's presence. Though I had never seen anyone "fall in the Spirit," as I knelt there, in the presence of the Lord, the Holy Spirit just "took me out," and I lay on the floor. I knew I was at His feet, and I began to thank Him and praise Him. When I looked up, I saw Jesus standing there. He was as real to me as I believe He will be when I get to heaven, though I may see Him differently then. I am sure the Holy Spirit revealed Him to me as He would have looked while in His human body.

As He stood at my feet, I thought that He must be in His glorified body, but I felt I was seeing Him as He looked when He was on the earth. I have never forgotten the impression it made on me.

Ever since that vision of Jesus, when I look at paintings that try to depict Him I think sadly, *They missed it*. His eyes were so penetrating that it seemed as if He looked through me. His mouth was not a grin, but a glow of pleasantness, though He was very serious. He had broad shoulders and seemed so strong.

When He blessed me, He said I would know a love I had never known. I know what love is, because I experienced it then and since then from His own hands. It far surpasses human love. As I beheld Him I understood why children felt comfortable with Him.

His physique was not outstanding. In my vision He had dark auburn hair and the deepest blue eyes I have ever looked into in my life. He had an olive complexion, and I remember that I was surprised, though I shouldn't have been. It had never dawned on me that when Jesus walked the earth He was a Jew and would have had an olive complexion. I said to Him, "I didn't know You had that kind of complexion."

He responded, "But I was a Jew."

While I was in the vision (it was not a vision to me, but a literal encounter), I talked to Him as I would have to another person, and He talked to me. Looking at me with those penetrating eyes, He said, "I want you to give Me your mind."

How do I do that? I thought. The Holy Spirit prompted me mentally to take my mind in my hands as though it were a cranium and to hand it to Jesus. He blessed it and said, "'Let this mind be in you, which was also in Christ Jesus' (Phil 2:5). You will know things you have never known. As you yield your mind to Me, I will give you My mind." And He blessed my mind and gave it back to me.

Then He said, "Now give me your ears." In the vision I handed Him my ears. He blessed them and said, "You shall hear My voice and know what the Spirit hath to say." Then He handed them back to me and asked me to give Him my mouth. I handed Him my mouth, and He blessed it and said, "You will speak words you have never spoken. They will not be your words but words of truth that I shall speak through your mouth."

Then He said, "Give me your eyes." When I gave them to Him, He said something that stunned me: "You shall see things that the prophets desired to see and could not see."

Somehow He communicated to me that this promise was not because of my goodness, but because the prophets were not living during the time when they could see what I would be privileged to see.

When He finished, I realized I had just committed three of my natural senses—sight, hearing, and tasting—to God in an act of consecration. Then He said to me, "Now give me your body."

(Though this was a deeply sacred moment, I have to tell it like it happened.) I responded, "I thought my body belonged to my husband, George. The Bible says that in marriage our bodies belong to our spouse (1 Cor. 7:4)." The presence of the Lord was so awesome that I thought He was asking me for complete ownership and that I could not belong to my husband.

The Lord replied, "If you will give Me your body, I will teach you a love you have never known that will allow you to love your husband like you never have." I consecrated my body to the Lord in that moment, and I can truthfully say that for the last five years of our marriage before my husband went to be with the Lord, He gave me a love that I did not dream existed between a man and woman. We enjoyed ecstasy in the sanctification of our marriage that we did not know was possible.

The Lord then asked me to give Him my hands. He moved to my side and picked them up. He didn't say much about my hands. He simply took them in His hands. He blessed my hands without saying anything about them. He laid them back down and walked back to my feet, and He asked me to hand them to Him. I picked up my feet, and He blessed them and said, "These feet shall walk paths you have never dreamed. You will go places where you have never thought you would go." Forty years later, I stand in awe of the fact that I have been in forty-seven of these United States and have traveled to most of the other continents as well to minister the gospel.

Then the Lord walked back to my side and asked for my hands again. I gave them to Him again, and He looked at them. This time He said, "I am going to teach you how to pray for the sick."

I began to cry. I said, "Lord, I can't pray for the sick. Oral Roberts does that." As I watched, He took my hands and laid them on the ears of a little boy. I looked, and standing beside me stood a little dark-haired boy perhaps ten years of age.

Jesus didn't tell me anything about the little boy. He just began to teach me what to say when I prayed for the sick. He said, "In the name of Jesus." Then He asked me, "What did Jesus say to the devil?"

"It is written," I replied.

Then He said, "By the power of the blood, and by My Spirit, through faith in My name."

He taught me to use these five weapons for receiving deliverance and healing against the power of the enemy. He taught me this lesson again when He gave me a vision of David. I understood that He has given us His *name,* His *blood,* His *Word,* His *Spirit,* and His *faith* to use as weapons to gain victory over the enemy.

After He had given me the weapons, the Lord said to me, "You can't do this yourself."

I started to cry again, embarrassed that He thought I would think I could do it on my own. I said to Him tearfully, "I know I can't. I don't know how. I couldn't do it anyway."

He continued gently, "I want you to know you will not be doing this. I will do it through your hands and through your mouth." Then He repeated, "In My name, by My blood, by My Spirit, by My Word, and through My faith."

He wanted me to understand that it was not through my faith that I would see healings take place. I cannot accept the teaching of a faith healing that teaches we are responsible for our own faith to be healed. That is not what He taught me. He reminded me of what Paul declared in Galatians 2:20: " . . . the life which I now live in the flesh I live by the faith of the Son of God, who loved me, and gave himself for me." All faith, even saving faith, comes from God (Eph. 2:8). He wanted me to understand that the tools He had given us for victory came from Him—His name, His Word, His blood, His Spirit, and His faith.

As my hands were laid on that little boy in the vision, I repeated those five weapons to him one by one. I didn't see anything happen to him; I was simply learning how to pray from the words of Jesus to me.

Then, as He walked back to my feet once again, He blessed me and said, "Now you can say you are my *doulos.*"

Doulos is the Greek word for *bondservant* or *love slave,* one who will do what the Master asks, when He asks, without question, without information, without reservation, or further revelation.

The Lord said to me, "Now you are my *doulos,* and you may call Me *Master.*"

I realized this was the first time in my life that He had known He was my Master, the Master of this temple. Then He looked at me and smiled the sweetest smile.

The experience of this vision of consecration must have continued for an hour or more. I didn't tell anybody. I could only cry in His presence. I continued talking to Him during the vision, though I was awestruck at what was happening. It was a private thing between Him and me. I realized that I had learned what the word *surrender* or *consecration* meant. He was now my Master, and I was His servant in a new way.

The Vision Fulfilled

THE NEXT MORNING I went back to the Atlanta church to minister. Brother Byrd spoke to the congregation, without saying one word to me, and told them, "Tonight we are going to have a healing service, and Sister Parrish is going to help us pray for the sick." I almost fell off the chair. I wanted to say *no*. But then I remembered my vision of the night before. I looked at Reverend Byrd and thought, *Who told you?*

In the service that night he gave an invitation to those who wanted prayer for healing. I thought a few people would come for prayer. As I watched people respond to the invitation, I saw that a line was stretched across the entire church and down the side aisle. I sensed a feeling of panic inside.

I comforted myself with the thought that the pastor and his elders were with me. However, when I stood to begin praying for the people, the pastor disappeared. I looked around for him and heard the elders say to me, "Go ahead."

The first one in line to be prayed for was a little boy. I didn't think to ask him what was wrong with him. I didn't know I was supposed to. I just took my hands and put them on his ears and tried to say exactly what Jesus had taught me to say in the vision. I said, "In the name of Jesus, by the power of the blood, and the authority of the written Word, by the power of the Spirit, and through His faith. . . ."

My hands were on his head, and I realized suddenly that I was holding the ears that I had held in the vision. I stopped praying and said to him, "Tell your mommy you love Jesus."

He turned around and said to the woman standing beside him, "I love Jesus."

In that instant she let out a war whoop and screamed. I did not know that the little boy had been completely deaf.

His mother was a Lutheran woman who had seen the announcement in the paper that there would be prayer for the sick that night. She was beside herself with joy, though not accustomed to such ecstatic expressions in church.

I learned that they were not even from Atlanta but had come to admit the child to Emory University for surgery on his ears the following Friday. His eardrums were ruptured, and they were going to operate on one of his ears that week and on the other a week later to replace the destroyed eardrums with plastic ones.

The following Friday night she came back to the church with a paper from a doctor at Emory University that confirmed that both the boy's eardrums were normal.

A LASTING TESTIMONY

YEARS LATER WHEN I was pastoring Fountaingate Church in Dallas, a church that we had founded, I received a wonderful surprise one Monday, a day when we were usually off and away from the office. That day we were at the church working in the nursery, painting, and renovating. I was trying to be a good pastor and do the work the people did. So I got into painting, much to their regret. They had to buy a lot of paint when I was painting.

I was wearing an old paint dress that day and had paint all over me. The secretary buzzed the phone in the nursery and said there was someone there who wanted to see me. I refused. "Tell him to come back tomorrow."

She said, "He can't come tomorrow. He is from out of town. He says he needs to see you. I told him you were painting, and he said that doesn't matter."

I relented, reluctantly, and said, "All right, send him on back."

A few minutes later, a handsome young man over six-feet tall walked into the nursery where I was painting. He said, "Sister Parrish, I mean Sister Pickett, they tell me you are married again."

I answered politely, "Yes, I am Sister Pickett. Mr. Parrish passed away in 1963."

"You don't know me," he continued, smiling. "I am the little boy who was deaf that you prayed for in Atlanta. I am home on furlough from the mission field in Brazil."

Overcome with joy, I slid off the stool I was sitting on and stood on the floor. I looked up at him and asked, "Did you know you were the first person I ever prayed for to be healed?"

We rejoiced together at the goodness of God and His faithfulness to us.

At the time I did not know that these were only the first lessons I would be taught by the Spirit of God in special visitations that brought revelation of the ways of God to my heart. The lessons continued, giving me understanding of the kingdom of God and of His victory over the enemy. ∾

Six

Humbled by Fresh Revelation

I WAS MINISTERING AT a Pentecostal church in High Point, North Carolina, when I heard the Lord's voice at the end of one of my messages. He said to me, "Sit down a minute." I sat down, and then He asked me, "Would you like to know what happened to you when you were born again?"

I remember feeling a little embarrassed and even insulted. I thought, *Have I walked this long with God without understanding what happened to me when I got saved?* I had acknowledged my dumbness about other areas of truth, but surely I understood something as basic as salvation. But I sat down in obedience to His voice, and as I did the Holy Spirit opened a vision to me.

He showed me Mary, the mother of Jesus, when she knelt in the presence of an angel. As the angel

Gabriel told her not to be afraid and continued his divine message to her, telling her she would conceive and bring forth a son and call His name *Jesus,* Mary said to the angel, "How shall this be, seeing I know not a man? And the angel answered and said unto her, The Holy Ghost shall come upon thee, and the power of the Highest shall overshadow thee: therefore also that holy thing which shall be born of thee shall be called the Son of God" (Luke 1:34–35).

Mary was clothed with a cloud of glory as the Holy Spirit brought the incorruptible seed—the eternal Word of God—and planted it in her uterus. After Mary had conceived, she said, "My soul doth magnify the Lord, and my spirit hath rejoiced in God my Saviour." As I watched the vision unfold before me, the Holy Spirit explained to me what had actually transpired in my spirit when I was born again.

I had understood and accepted salvation through the terms "saved" and "born again"—both biblical terms. But the Holy Spirit made me understand that what the Holy Spirit did in Mary, impregnating her with the living seed of God, He had done in my spirit in salvation. The incorruptible seed of God— His living Word—was placed in my spirit when I was born again, and I was impregnated with the life of Christ. I have shared this revelation with people who have been walking with God for twenty years, and they tell me they did not understand what had happened to them in salvation.

I understood more clearly then the Scripture, "Christ in you, the hope of glory" (Col. 1:27). Christ in me is a reality, not a philosophical analogy. I understand, of course, that it means Christ in *all* of you, the body of Christ, and not in just one believer. The life of Christ will be expressed completely through His body, the church. But the truth of His life in me became a reality to me that night.

The incorruptible seed that Peter refers to in his epistle is Christ Himself, impregnating our spirit with His life—the living Word of God. (See 1 Peter 1:23.) I saw that He must increase within us and bring forth His life through our spirits into our minds and emotions, pushing out the carnal life that was dead in trespasses and sins, as we continually yield to Him.

I bowed my head in awe that day and said sorrowfully to Him, "I have walked with You for seventeen years and taught Your Word without really understanding what had happened to me in salvation." I asked Him, "Why didn't You tell me before? Why did You wait almost twenty years to tell me?"

I heard Him say so sweetly, "You don't tell babies the facts of life until they are old enough to understand. You don't explain to a baby that he was a seed in his mother's uterus. You say just enough to a young child to satisfy him until he gets old enough to comprehend." He explained, "You weren't old enough in Me to comprehend the wonder of the born-again reality."

It was after this experience that the Holy Spirit began to open my understanding about being impregnated with the Word of God. With His revelation I was able to begin ministering that life of Christ when I preached. That was very different from the years of study from an intellectual approach before I received the baptism of the Holy

Spirit. Later, as He revealed the Book of Esther to me in vision form, I would understand more about being "lifed" by the Word.

REVELATION OF "IN CHRIST"

IT IS A PRECIOUS truth that once we come into divine revelation of the Word, unless we willfully walk away from God, that revelation will continue to flow to us. I discovered that the Holy Spirit would take me to class for instruction at some of the most unexpected times.

One morning as I was on my way to the church to pray, there was a traffic accident, and all the red lights were thrown out of sync for several minutes. We were forced to sit in traffic, and no one knew exactly how long we would be detained.

Rather than allow this interruption to my plans to irritate me, I began to pray. Sirens screamed as traffic backed up for miles at the red lights. But I decided to praise the Lord instead of fussing about having to sit there.

As I began to turn my attention to the goodness of God, my Teacher spoke these words to me, "God in Christ, Christ in God, Christ in the Holy Ghost, the Holy Ghost in Christ." He went through each member of the Godhead, combining them back and forth. Then He said, "And all three of them in you."

I shook my head in bewilderment. I said, "I don't know what you are saying. That sounds complicated to me." He repeated patiently, "God is in Christ. Christ is in God. Christ is in the Holy Ghost. The Holy Ghost is in Christ." Soon the traffic was moving again, and I drove on to the church. When I arrived, I bowed at the altar. I asked Him to explain what He had been talking to me about as I drove to the church.

I heard Him say, "In [Christ] dwelleth all the fulness of the Godhead bodily" (Col. 2:9). Then He said, "God dwells in Christ. Christ dwells in God. The Holy Ghost dwells in God." And I began to see the triune Godhead rather than three separate entities—or "members"—of the trinity. Then He said, "The Godhead dwells in Christ; Christ dwells in you; Christ in you the hope of glory."

I was still having a hard time understanding the significance of what the Holy Spirit was showing me. As I continued kneeling there that day, the Holy Spirit told me to get my sand bucket. I said aloud to Him, "I don't have a sand bucket."

He said, "Darrell has one—get that one." I remembered that when my son Darrell was small, he had a big sand bucket. I recalled vividly the day he fell on the metal shovel that went with the bucket and cut his forehead. It was a frightening experience for all of us.

In the vision that began to unfold I got Darrell's sand bucket, and then the Holy Spirit said, "Now, come and go with Me." So I went with Him down to the ocean. As I stood looking at that vast expanse of water, He said, "Dip your bucket into the ocean and fill it full." I did and pulled up my bucket, full of water. Then we started back up the hill. He said, "What do you have in the bucket?"

I answered simply, "The ocean."

He said, "Rightly so. Every component part of that ocean is in your bucket."

The Holy Spirit continued, "You can take the

water in that bucket to a laboratory to test it, and every mineral and element that is in the ocean is in that bucket." My thoughts went to a familiar principle from my nursing background—hematology, which explains how one drop of blood can tell the story of all the blood in a person's body. I began to understand how all of Christ can be in us. None of us have all of Him. But we can have all He is— every component part.

I understood that I didn't need the whole ocean to have Christ in me—I just needed a bucketful. But then He said to me, "Turn around and look again. What do you see?"

I said, "The ocean."

Then He asked again, "What do you have in your bucket?"

"The ocean."

"Do you want what is in your bucket or what you see?"

Without hesitation I declared, "I want that," pointing to the vast body of water in front of me.

"Then take your bucket and go jump in."

In the vision I jumped into that ocean with my bucket bobbing up and down beside me. As I looked, I saw a lot of other buckets bobbing up and down. Then the Holy Spirit explained, "As your bucket was in the ocean, and the ocean was in the bucket, so God is in you, and you are in God." He was telling me that the triune Godhead not only lives in heaven, but each member of the Godhead lives in me as well.

I considered the declaration of Jesus, "Blessed are the pure in heart, for they shall see God." I used to think that meant we would go to heaven and be with God if we kept our hearts pure. But now I understand we can see God with our spiritual eyes by revelation now, before heaven. After all those years of teaching the Word, it dawned on me that Christ Jesus is not just up there on the throne hearing me when I pray. He lives in me literally—all of the Godhead bodily—Christ in me, the hope of glory, is a reality.

MYSTERY OF THE TRINITY

SEVERAL YEARS AGO when I started writing my first book, *God's Dream,* which related God's eternal plan for mankind, I began to understand more fully that the members of the trinity are not as separated as we have taught. The Godhead is united.

Many theologians have taught dispensationally that God the Father initiated the Law. Then Jesus came to initiate the dispensation of grace, and when He ascended to heaven, the Holy Ghost came to usher in another dispensation. Many teach that Christ is now seated at the right hand of the Father and the Holy Ghost is on earth to do His work.

Of course that is true, but that is not all there is. God was in Christ as He walked the earth, and Christ is in us because of the new birth. We have been taught that Christ showed us the Father while He was on earth, that the Father was in heaven and Christ on the earth. But Christ was not simply showing us an *example* of who the Father is. The Father was in Christ while He was on the earth, so that Christ Himself was a revelation of the Father.

When Jesus' disciples asked Him to reveal the Father to them, His reply was full of pathos: "If ye had known me, ye should have known my Father also: and from henceforth ye know him, and have seen him" (John 14:7). There is a reality of relationship in that statement that many of us have not grasped. We have separated the Godhead too completely, limiting each member to the time and space that limits us as finite human beings.

I believe that we are going to know God in a way we don't yet know Him in the days ahead. Many have not realized that He lives in us. They pray to God way up yonder and relegate Christ to sitting at the right hand of the Father. Though He does sit at the right hand of the Father in His glorified body, He is not limited to that "place." I can pray to Him, knowing that He also is in me to live His life through me.

And He is in you as well—His church, His body. Only by revelation can we break the time and space barriers of our thinking to understand the wonder of the Godhead dwelling in heaven and in us—each of us who believe on Him. By allowing Him to fill our buckets and then jumping into the ocean, we can experience the living water that He is to us. That will allow us to be a part of the wonderful reservoir that He is filling up with His Word and to find our place in the reaping of the great End-Time harvest. ∿

Seven

Power Over the Enemy

ON ANOTHER OCCASION, I was again praying before I went to bed one Wednesday night in the home where I was a guest. The Lord came to me again and said, "If you will spend the night with Me, as the day dawns into the morning I will teach you how to have power over the devil." You can be sure I did not sleep that night. I was sitting on the daybed by the window in my host's den watching for the day to break, for the Lord had said, "As the day dawns, I will teach you." (It is important that you understand that I had never learned any of these truths in my years of studying theology or in pastoring and teaching the Word. I had not even been exposed to Pentecostal people or doctrine.)

I sat there, waiting for more special instructions from my Teacher—the Holy Spirit. Just as the dawn began to crack the tiniest bit, someone walked into my room. It was as though I was in a trance or being transported to another place. I looked up, and there was a young man with broad shoulders and a ruddy face. He had something strange slung over his shoulder. He looked as though he had been outdoors a lot. He was strong, but he wasn't mammoth or tall—just a nice physique.

I realized he was not a young boy, but perhaps in his late teens. My attention was drawn to the cloth on his shoulder. The Holy Spirit said to me, "That is a shepherd's sling." I had never seen a sling like the kind that was used in Bible days, but always thought of our version of slingshots that boys used to shoot at birds. I didn't know what a shepherd's sling looked like before that night. I have since studied what they look like and have found they are part of a robe that is worn draped around the body. With part of it you can kill the enemy, and part of it is used to cover you. When I visited the Holy Land years after this vision, I actually saw a shepherd's sling such as the one I saw on the shoulder of this young man in my vision.

As I looked at him, I said, "You are David!" You can't imagine how I felt—a little Methodist woman sitting there seeing David. It was difficult for my intellect to grasp what I was experiencing, though my spirit responded eagerly.

Then the Lord said to me, "Watch him." And I began to watch a drama unfold.

There was a brook at David's feet. He reached down and picked up five stones and held them in his hand. I saw the stones, and I saw the brook. I knew the Bible story.

About that time, a huge person walked into the other side of the room. I looked up, startled by his size, and whispered, "You are a giant." In that instant I realized that he was Goliath. The Spirit said to me, "He is nine-feet three-inches tall." (Later I learned that is the height the Bible records for Goliath.) As I sat there spellbound by the drama unfolding before me, I looked at the giant and then looked over at David.

The Holy Spirit spoke to me again, "I will teach you how to have power over the devil. Watch David." As I did, I saw him put away four of the stones in his hand. He took one and put it in the sling that was on his shoulder. My Teacher asked me, "In what did he come and throw that rock?"

I answered, "In the name of the Lord of hosts."

As I said that, David picked up the rock and slung it at the giant, hitting him in the forehead. I watched as that mammoth man fell. Then the Spirit said to me, "Now you get up and pick up the other four rocks." And, in the vision, He let Goliath stand back up.

Now *I* had to use these stones to defeat him. This was the second time He taught me about the weapons He had given us to defeat the enemy. The Holy Spirit asked me, "What stone did Jesus throw at the devil?" (Then I understood that Goliath was a type of Satan.)

I declared, "Jesus' response to the devil was, 'It is written.' He threw the Word at the devil." As I stood there in the middle of the den, whirling my sling and throwing that stone, I hit Goliath, and he reeled and started down. But he didn't go all the way down. The Holy Spirit was letting me fight the enemy now.

Then the Spirit asked me, "What is the line that the enemy cannot cross?"

I said, "The blood of Jesus. He cannot cross the blood."

He said, "Take that stone and throw it." There I was, a dignified former Methodist professor, standing in the middle of the room throwing rocks from my shepherd's sling. If someone would have opened the door and seen me, they would have been astonished at the sight.

As I threw the stone that represented the blood, the giant went down again—but he got up part of the way.

Then the Spirit asked, "In whose strength do you fight?"

I raised my arm, and it felt like it had hundreds of pounds of strength. I declared, "Not by might, nor by power, but by my spirit, saith the Lord of hosts" (Zech. 4:6). I understood we had to move by the power of the Holy Spirit.

The four stones I had used so far to defeat the enemy were His name, His Word, His blood, and the power of His Spirit.

I had one rock left. By that time Goliath was almost finished. He barely got his head back up.

Then the Holy Spirit asked me, "Whose faith is it?"

I declared with Paul, "The life which I now live in the flesh I live by the faith of the Son of God" (Gal. 2:20), and threw that last rock at the giant. When I threw that rock, the enemy was totally defeated with no strength to rise again.

As the Holy Spirit taught me that morning, He made sure that I understood the names of those stones—the same weapons He had taught me to use in the vision when He showed me how to pray for the sick.

Defeating the enemy is not about standing and yelling and stomping our feet. It involves using the divine arsenal of weapons God has given us—the name of the Lord, His Word, His blood, the power of His Spirit, and His faith. These are all He tells us to use to come against Satan.

Then the Spirit said to me, "Put those five stones in the sling of praise and go conquer the enemy."

I was unaware of my surroundings or the time of day during this classroom session with my Teacher. But morning had come, and my host, Brother Jackson, had awakened and come into the room. When he saw me, he left immediately, closed the door, and said to his wife, Lola, "I want you to take the telephone off the hook and lock the door. Don't let anyone in this house today. God has that woman, and we are not going to disturb her." The whole house was filled with the presence of the Lord as my Teacher continued to reveal the Word to me.

WHAT IS A DEMON?

EVERY FRIDAY MORNING a healing service in the Atlanta church was attended by people from all over the city. One Friday morning, after the vision on Wednesday night, Pastor Byrd had to go to the hospital to pray for a deacon. He asked me to teach and then pray for the sick that day, assuring me that the elders would be there and I would be safe.

So I taught that Friday morning and then asked reluctantly if anyone needed prayer for healing. People started coming to the front of the church for prayer. At the front of the line stood a quiet little woman, not quite five-feet tall. I had seen her in the services. She seemed to be a sweet lady. As she stood there waiting for prayer, however, the look on her face changed from sweetness to an ugly snarl, and when she stepped up in front of me she yelled, "I will kill you!"

Startled, I looked into her contorted face and heard her yell again, "I will kill her, and I will kill you!"

I didn't have time to get scared. I responded loudly and firmly, "You will not! You will go back to darkness where you came from, in the name of Jesus. You will kill nobody, and you will not kill her!" I was taught in my home that a lady was always to speak softly, not to yell at people. I had never spoken to anyone in the authoritative tone of voice that I used that day.

Suddenly, as I spoke, that little woman fell at my feet with a thud, as though she were dead. I just stood there, not knowing what to do next. The elders were standing there watching me. I thought, *What have I done?*

I had never seen a demon before. They taught me in Bible college that there were no demons in America. I remember a missionary to China who spoke to us in a chapel service and related what they did in China to tear down idols and cast out demons. But we understood that a pastor in America did not have to deal with demons. So you can imagine my surprise when I heard myself rebuking a demon in Jesus' name.

After a few moments the lady looked up at me, smiled, and said, "I love you."

She was just as free and sweet as she had appeared to me before the devil manifested himself. She stood up erect before me. I didn't know the woman had suffered with rheumatoid arthritis all through her body. In the moment the devil left her, she was completely healed as well.

The following Christmas I went back to Atlanta to visit. As I walked into the church, a lady walked up to greet me. She said, "Hello, Sister Parrish. You don't remember me, do you? I am the little woman that had the demon that said he was going to kill you." She smiled the sweetest smile. She looked beautiful—with a shining countenance and healthful appearance.

That was my first encounter with a demon. I had not had any lessons about casting out a demon. Though my lesson with David taught me how to confront the enemy, I never expected to have to confront a demon because of the way I had been taught. It was the name of Jesus that destroyed its power over the woman.

"I'M ONE OF THEM"

ON THE SUNDAY morning following that eventful Friday morning healing service, I first heard people sing and praise in tongues corporately. The guest speaker, Dr. Phillips from England, asked the congregation to stand and praise God. Over a thousand people stood and sang in tongues. I remember wondering if it was right to sing in tongues. It was all still so new to me.

Dr. Phillips had deferred to me, saying he wanted to hear a lady preach. While I was preaching, I began to sing an original melody spontaneously under the anointing, "I'm one of them, I'm one of them. I'm so glad that I can say, I'm one of them."

In that moment the Lord reminded me that when I passed a Pentecostal church I used to say, "I'm glad I am *not* one of them." On the day I was healed, He had asked me if I would be willing to identify with these people. I had said *yes*, and now I was rejoicing in that commitment.

As I stood singing, "I'm one of them, I'm one of them. I'm so glad that I can say, I'm one of them," the church began to sing with me. And it dawned on me—I *was* one of them! I was no longer a woman without a country. God had made me one of His Pentecostal people—a people I had despised for years.

REMOVING A DEMON

AFTER THE SERVICE that morning I was planning to go to lunch with some friends when the Spirit spoke to me, "If you will spend the afternoon with Me, I will teach you what a demon is."

I said, "All right."

So I asked the ladies to excuse me from lunch, telling them that I needed to stay and get ready for the evening service. Then I went to my room and stretched out across the bed. I wasn't really praying. I just said, "Lord, I am with You."

Suddenly, the Holy Spirit opened to me a vision in which I was taken into a hospital. I was a part of the vision, and I was wheeling a patient into the operating room. Hospitals were not strange to me because I had practiced nursing for eight years. While I was studying in Bible college, I studied nursing as well, thinking I would be sent to the mission field. (One of my great fears as a young Christian was that I would have to go to Africa as a missionary, where I would be eaten by the snakes. But I finally made a complete surrender that whether I lived or died, I would rather be in Africa than to die out of the will of God in a New York penthouse.) The Holy Spirit was about to draw on my knowledge of nursing to give me an analogy of what a demon was.

I enjoyed nursing and had volunteered for two terms instead of the one term required as an assistant in the operating room. I had watched many operations, observed the procedures, and knew, in many cases, what the doctors were supposed to do at each step.

In the vision, after I wheeled the patient into the operating room, I saw the man from oncology, who had come in to take a blood sample, and an x-ray technician, who turned on the light and hung up the x-ray. It was a very intense light, located at the head of the patient, and it illuminated that x-ray clearly. The doctors and technicians all stood looking intently at the x-ray. They had studied it before, but, at the moment of surgery, they were looking at it again so that their procedure would be precise.

I wasn't quite sure what I was watching. What did this operating room scene have to do with a demon? Then the Holy Spirit spoke to me, "I want you to watch this operation closely. The doctors do not proceed casually with the operation. They have carefully diagnosed the problem and are ready to correct it."

As I watched the surgeon standing over the patient while still looking at the x-ray, the Spirit asked me, "What is the surgeon going after?"

I answered, "He is looking for a foreign body."

He responded, "That is correct. And that is what a demon is—a foreign body that is usurping or leeching off a human being." I understood that He was comparing a physical foreign body to a demon, which is a spiritual foreign body that preys on men's souls.

He continued, "The surgeon and staff are going in to extricate the foreign body. But they are not going after it without knowledge. They are following strict procedure based on the evidence they have of what is wrong with the patient."

As the vision continued to unfold, I watched the procedure. They put the patient to sleep and then began, step by step, to skillfully remove that foreign body. I have remembered this vision when I have been in situations where people are screaming at the devil, asking him to tell his name, and going through other emotional gyrations to cast out a demon. The surgeon and his team were resolved, prepared, and skillful in the removal of the foreign body from their patient.

Once I saw the surgeon stop and confer with his colleagues about what they were seeing. And I could imagine Jesus and the Holy Spirit comparing notes as They do Their work of redeeming a soul. The assisting technicians were not standing as spectators in that operating room. All eyes were looking intently at the source of the disease, cooperating fully with the surgeon.

The analogy was clear. A demon was a foreign

body that attached itself to a human soul and would destroy him or her if not removed. But it cannot be removed promiscuously; it must be removed carefully. The surgeon had to know what it was and how to go after it. And he worked in complete unity with the team in the operating room.

As soon as the foreign body was removed, the patient was stitched carefully to help in his recovery. And the Spirit said to me, "Watch carefully the follow-up procedure to such a surgery." One of the technicians gave the patient a shot of penicillin to guard against infection. In the Bible, the hyssop was used to cleanse. David cried out, "Cleanse me with hyssop, and I will be clean" (Ps. 51:7, NIV). I had learned that penicillin is made from blue mold that comes from hyssop, and they told me hyssop is one of the strongest ingredients in penicillin.

It is important that in spiritual "surgery" we remember to apply the Word of God consistently to a recovering patient to avoid postoperative complications. Eradication of the foreign body is not enough to insure future victory in a person's life. Postoperative care is vital.

Then the doctors gave instructions to the nurses for caring for the patient after he was taken to his room. Too often we deliver a person of demonic powers and leave their "house"—soul—open and vulnerable to the return of worse evil. My mind went to the story Jesus told about the evil spirit coming back and finding the house swept clean—but empty—and bringing more evil spirits in to dwell there. (See Matthew 12:44-45.) We need to give the delivered instructions on how to close the door of the house to prevent further invasion of the enemy.

Still impacted with what I had seen that afternoon as the Holy Spirit revealed to me what a demon was and how to defeat it, I stood to preach that night and began to share the vision I had received. Dr. Adams, a physician who was listed in *Who's Who in Surgery in America,* was in the congregation. I did not know he was there. I'm glad I didn't, because I might have been intimidated as I tried to share medical terms and procedures. I was just a nurse. I described the operating room, the procedure as I had observed it, and the understanding I received about the need to use the right instrument at the right time when delivering people. It was not for unskilled people. All eyes were to be fastened on the chief surgeon, who was Jesus. And we were to cooperate with Him in caring for the patient.

The next morning the pastor called me and asked if I could go to lunch with someone.

I asked, "Do you want me to?"

"Yes, Dr. Adams would like to take you to lunch today. He wants to talk to you about the vision you shared last night." I trembled inwardly but consented to go.

As we ate lunch, Dr. Adams asked me questions about the vision I had shared. After we finished eating, he pushed his plate back, looked at me intently, and said, "Sister Parrish, I have never heard a more scientific description of deliverance from evil spirits. Last night was the first time I could agree that demons were real foreign bodies that needed to be extracted from a person's soul. I understand now that a demon is a foreign body that has come to kill. And it will kill if it is not removed, but it has to be done carefully." The Holy Spirit had given this medical doctor an analogy he could relate to in order to understand a spiritual truth.

Though I had taught classes on angels—classifying the kinds of good and bad angels there are—I had never learned how to cooperate with the Holy Spirit to deliver a captive soul from demonic power. The weapons He showed me to use in the bringing down of Goliath—His name, His blood, His Word, His Spirit, His faith—were attending instruments to be used skillfully.

To teach me how to use them specifically against demonic power in a person, the Holy Spirit had taken me to a familiar setting—the operating room. Then I understood how to care for a patient during surgery and afterward. I have seen patients die because they didn't have the right care after surgery. They needed antibiotics to kill the infection. The blood and the Word are like spiritual antibiotics for our souls. They bring healing to us.

A RECENT DELIVERANCE

A FEW MONTHS ago, I was ministering in Olen Griffing's church in Shady Grove, Texas. We had prayed for most of the congregation, and many were lying on the floor under the power of the Spirit. When I finished praying for people, I went to sit down. As I sat there observing the work of God in so many lives, two elders brought a man to me and asked me to help them pray for him.

As soon as I looked at the man, I knew his problem was demonic. I thought, *I am weary; why don't you folk pray for him?* Looking again at the man, I remembered the surgeon's procedure I had seen in the vision years before. I stood to pray for him and asked the elders to stand by me.

The man's eyes were glassy-looking, and he almost snarled at me. I said, "In the name of Jesus." We used the weapons we knew to use. But there was no change; he still stood looking at me with glassy eyes. So I sat down for a moment to regroup and prayed, "Lord, what next? What am I to do?"

The Lord spoke to me, "Tell him to pray in tongues."

I was startled. *What?* Tell a demonically controlled man to pray in tongues? I heard the Spirit say to me again clearly, "Tell him to pray in tongues. He has had the baptism and has grieved the Holy Spirit."

I stood back up and said with authority, "Sir, have you received the baptism of the Holy Spirit?"

He said, "Yes, ma'am."

"Pray in tongues," I commanded him. His response was garbled. I said again, "In the name of Jesus, pray in the language of the Spirit."

Suddenly he began to pray in tongues, and I recognized that his spirit had begun to pray. The Holy Spirit was washing all the bitterness from his soul, all the resentment and anger that were there. After a while his countenance began to beam with a divine glow. He had "prayed through." The last I saw of him he was praying in tongues and shouting.

I said to the elders, "I have never done that before." They were thrilled with their friend's deliverance. The man had grieved the Holy Spirit, and by surrendering his own human spirit back to the Holy Spirit he received divine deliverance from the demonic powers that tormented him.

Jesus is the one who does the surgery, by the power of the Holy Spirit. All we have to do is co-operate with Him. I was in awe of the specific direction I had received that was contrary to what I understood to do when dealing with demonic power. I sat there trembling. Later I consulted with the pastor to make sure people would not mis-understand why I had told someone troubled by demons to pray in tongues. (It is possible for demons to speak in tongues, as those involved in witchcraft have demonstrated.) The pastor con-firmed that the man we prayed for had had the baptism and walked with God until he allowed defeat to separate him. I have since heard that he is walking in victory and going on with God.

The understanding I received from the vision of David and the vision of the operating room became invaluable to me. The five weapons He has pro-vided for us to use against the devil are, of course, established in the Word of God. But knowing the power we have to use them gave wonderful hope to expect victory over every enemy.

I did not realize how graphic and literal the visions had been until I found myself taking a trip to the Holy Land some time later. It was while trav-eling there that I realized I had been there before, not physically, but with my spiritual eyes. It hum-bled me to know that God had revealed this to me in such a wonderful way. ∾

Eight

A New Phase of Ministry

FOR SEVERAL MONTHS I kept in touch with the church in Atlanta and was ministered to by the people there while traveling and preaching revivals in the area. Then, during one of the conferences I was attending there, the pastor said to me, "You are leaving now."

He had called the North Carolina District of the Assemblies of God and had recommended me to them. He said that I would not be a woman without a country now. They were willing to recognize my ministry, and I transferred my full ordination to become a part of their conference.

Before I left Atlanta, the leadership laid hands on me to send me out. The pastor prayed a prayer I have never forgotten. He prayed, "Jesus, for one year don't let her go where anyone will speak against what she has and what she is receiving from Your Word. Don't let anybody hurt her; don't let her go to a church where she will not be accepted. Protect her from opposition."

Later I thought, *Why did he pray that for only one year?* As I began to schedule meetings as far north as Ohio, the first year was glorious. Everywhere I went I felt accepted and enjoyed revival among the people. While ministering in Ohio, I first heard of Kathryn Kuhlman. We were near her home in Pittsburgh, and people shared about her powerful meetings. I had been so cloistered in a faith that I had not heard of her wonderful ministry of healing miracles.

While I was ministering in the north, a pastor said to me, "Do you know who you are?"

I answered hesitantly, not understanding his question, "Well, I am Fuchsia Parrish."

He replied, "No, God has brought an Esther to the kingdom for such a time as this." I had no time to be tempted to receive his remark as flattery, for he continued, "But it is not going to be easy for you. You are going to face opposition. But you have a message for the church." Then he prayed for me.

During that first year of traveling ministry, I did not encounter any real difficulties. I could say anything I wanted to say about what God had done for me and what I had received through revelation of the Word. I was well received wherever I went, and God moved in the meetings. I was ecstatic. I thought, *I have found my people. This is the Pentecostal movement, and I am accepted as one of them.* I was enjoying ministry in this new dimension.

On one occasion I was preaching in the church of a young preacher who was so hungry for the things of God. He was open to my message, and God was moving in the church. One night after the service, a little girl came to the altar and asked me to teach her how to receive the baptism. I thought I would teach her to love Jesus. So I said, "'Honey, let's just love the Lord, and He will give you the gift He has promised." I was holding her in my arms as I began to pray for her, and she was weeping.

Suddenly, I went out in the Spirit. I lost awareness of the little girl and fell out on the floor. I never knew when she received the baptism or when she left. As I lay there in the presence of God for several hours, the Holy Spirit revealed to me the persecution that was about to come.

The weather was hot, and there were mosquitoes buzzing around, but I was oblivious to my surroundings. The young pastor sat in the back of the church until the visitation was over about three o'clock the next morning. He could not know that as I lay there in a trance I was taking a trip through the Book of the Song of Solomon.

Up the mountains I went and smelled the spices and saw the gardens. It was wonderful. I was basking in the language of the Song of Solomon. "My beloved is gone down into his garden, to the beds of spices, to feed in the gardens, and to gather lilies" (Song of Sol. 6:2). I understood that He was gathering lilies for the wedding. Allegorically, I could see Him in the church. After enjoying His presence and the wonderful place of love and peace that is described in the Song of Solomon, I came to a place in the vision I did not understand or like.

It was a place of ditches and ravines. The path became rugged and continued past the garden up a terrible hill. In that moment, the Lord spoke to me and said, "You have to go that way."

I replied, "I don't want to. Do I have to?"

And He said, "Yes."

I was arguing inside myself: *You don't lead your bride that way.*

Then I heard Him say, "Come and go with me." And suddenly I was on a threshold, leaving this beautiful corridor and beautiful flowers and spices that I had enjoyed. I was heading for a rugged way. There was foliage on this way, but it wasn't pretty.

As I continued, a little bird came flying toward me. I had never seen a bird like that before. It was a tiny bird with very short feet and a long bill, and it was buzzing. It flew in a circular path and would take sweet nectar from nearby flowers and bring it and put it in my mouth. I thought, *This is wonderful.*

He continued flying to flowers to collect nectar and then bring it to me. Then one time when I tasted the nectar he brought, it was not sweet—it was bitter. I spit. I didn't want to swallow that. But the Lord spoke and said, "You will taste it. Come and go with Me."

I was curious about the little bird. I had never seen one like that before. I asked the Spirit what it was, and He said it was a hummingbird. I had never seen a hummingbird. Unexpectedly, I began to sing in tongues. When I did, the little bird came and started singing to me. Then I sang back to him in the Spirit. It was later that I understood he was tuning my spirit to get me ready to go where I was going. (As I later researched the little bird that had sung with me, I discovered that it was indeed a hummingbird, just as the Spirit had said.)

After the bird and I sang together, he flew up that rugged road, and I started following him. Everything I encountered was bitter and rugged. But I knew I was supposed to go. Later, I knew that this rugged path allegorically represented the path I was getting ready to walk into ministry.

After regaining consciousness of my surroundings, I sat up, and the pastor who was waiting for me said, "You have been lying there singing in tongues."

I replied, "I have never sung in tongues before."

He said, "Well, you did tonight."

PERSECUTION BEGINS

AT THE END of that first year, I was grateful that the prayers for my protection had been answered, but I soon wished that it covered more than one year. It was after that first year that, as I shared some of the revelations I had received, I began to receive persecution from some ministers. I was experiencing the fulfillment of the vision in which I had been led through a rugged, uphill path.

When I first began to receive revelation of the Scriptures, I thought *I* was the new baby—and that all the other Pentecostal preachers in the churches where I was ministering already knew what I was learning. I thought they would add to my revelation and help me to increase understanding of the little bit of truth I was seeing for the first time.

I would go to them with my revelation and tearfully say, "Look what I saw today." But instead of affirmation, many looked at me strangely, and then remarked to one another, "She is excited now, but she will cool off." I was taken aback by their response. Still, I kept studying the Word under the guidance of my new Teacher, the Holy Spirit, and living in awe of what I was understanding.

After being so well received for the first year of my traveling ministry, I felt confident that I could share the things God continued to show me from His Word without fear. So when I stood in a church in Hatteras, North Carolina, and announced that the next evening I was going to share some things that God had revealed to me in His Word, and I did, I was surprised at the negative response I received. The next day a presbyter called the pastor and said, "Don't let her preach those experiences she is having. If she does, it will cause people to seek experiences only instead of seeking God."

Some Pentecostal people were saying that what I had received by revelation was spurious. Until then, I didn't know that anybody in Pentecost believed any differently from what they taught in the Atlanta church. I had been to many other churches where I had such a good time rejoicing and sharing that I was shocked at this latest response.

Suddenly, none of the precious revelations I had received were "real." I was confronted with words like "balance" and "order." Ministers argued, "We don't walk that way. That's out in left field." I was hearing these comments from ministers within the denomination I had felt was God's will for me to become a part of. My world began to divide between those who were for my ministry totally and those who were questioning it.

The opposition was not attacking my character, but it was attacking the precious revelation I was receiving and the way I ministered the Word. I realized that I was seeing a line of demarcation—that there was a difference between ministering in the Spirit by revelation and ministering what you know by the intellect. Though I was hurt by the rejection of some, I received blessed acceptance by those ministers who know the ways of the Spirit. I realized that the bitter nectar I had tasted from the little bird was the opposition I was now experiencing.

I decided to walk on with the Lord. But because of that specific persecution, I locked up all the precious experiences of revelation that I had received. For years I did not share many of them. Once in a while I would share part of an experience with some of my students whom I trusted to receive it well. But I did not share the revelations openly in great detail as I had received them.

ADVENTURES IN THE HOLY LAND

DURING THIS SEASON, I was standing in my kitchen one morning when I heard the Lord say to me, "You are going to the West Coast." I had just finished a meeting in Winston-Salem, North Carolina, and had returned home to Eden, North Carolina. The meetings had been wonderful. I was initially invited for one week of meetings, which extended to six weeks. At the end of six weeks, several churches joined together and asked me if I would remain as the speaker for a citywide revival in a large, rented auditorium.

But the Lord told me to close the meeting and go home. He said, "Render unto Caesar the things that are Caesar's."

I didn't understand, yet I told the pastor that I was sorry, but I felt the Lord had spoken to me to close the meeting on Sunday. He was disappointed, but he agreed I should obey what I felt was God's will.

My husband had been joining me on the weekends, driving from our home in Greensboro, North Carolina, to Winston-Salem after finishing his week at work. He was a beautiful singer and would minister in song in the meetings. I called him and asked him not to come this weekend since I would be closing the meeting and returning home.

When I was alone I pondered what the Lord had said. What could "render unto Caesar the things that are Caesar's" mean? I didn't owe the government any money as far as I knew. I closed the meeting and went home.

On Monday morning I asked my husband, "Do we owe the government any taxes? Is something wrong? I've come home with a commission to render unto Caesar the things that are Caesar's. And I don't know what I am supposed to do."

He confirmed that we did not owe the government. He did not understand the Lord's words to me, either.

The next morning I was in my kitchen putting away some dishes when I heard the Lord speak to me, saying, "I will meet you in Jerusalem."

Startled, I asked, "What?"

He said, "Go apply for your visa. You are going to the Holy Land. You can go to the conference."

Then I understood that to render to Caesar in this situation was to get the government's permission to travel to the Holy Land.

For several months before that, I had been

praying about attending a Pentecostal conference in Jerusalem that I had seen advertised in a Christian periodical. I wanted to go so badly. But I had forgotten about it. That was the last week I could get a visa for the trip.

I heard the Lord say that morning, "I want you to go to Jerusalem, and I will introduce you to the man who will introduce you to the man who will open the doors for you on the West Coast."

Though I didn't have the money for that kind of trip and didn't have a visa or a passport, I obeyed what I had heard and went to the visa office that day. I applied for a passport and had just enough time to get it.

Then I called the office that was handling the tour group of nine hundred people going to the Holy Land and asked them to add my name to the group.

They replied, "There is no room for you."

I was undaunted because the Lord had said, "You are going." So I asked to be placed on a cancellation list and hung up.

Then I announced to my friends and family that I was going to the Holy Land. As I look back now, I can see how presumptuous I must have seemed. But it was really faith working. I told my mother I was going, and I got my things ready to go. I didn't have a ticket, visa, passport, or money to go. In a few days the passport and visa came. Ten days before departure I still had not heard from the tour group that there was room for me to go. But I announced I was going anyway.

Thelma and Hazel, two of my friends who had worked with me during the revivals, gave me a bon voyage party—they took me to dinner with a group of friends and gave me a gift. On the Saturday afternoon before the departure date, my friend Thelma came to visit. Soon after she arrived, Hazel drove into the driveway. She asked Thelma, "Is Fuchsia here?"

Thelma responded, "Yes." Then she asked, "Is she going to the Holy Land?"

Hazel answered, "I know she is going. But I wonder if she knows how."

She parked, got out of her car, and walked into the house. She said, "Hi, Fuchsia, I just came by to say hello." Then she said quietly to Thelma, "Tell her to look on the desk when I leave."

After Hazel left, I looked on my desk; there was a check for twelve hundred dollars—more than I needed for the entire trip to the Holy Land. I learned later that she had been saving for some furniture for her house and gave the money to me as a gift instead to make the trip.

Now I had everything I needed—passport, visa, and money—except for a plane ticket. I picked up my phone and called the travel agent.

He said again, "There is no room."

I replied, "Sir, I don't know you, but I will tell you one thing. A God who can give me a check this big for airfare has a seat for me on that plane. Please put me on standby. I am going with you."

On Monday afternoon, my husband, George, was mowing the lawn when he saw a telegraph boy coming up the drive. George called to me and said, "There is a little telegraph boy here who wants you to sign for something."

I looked at the letter. It was from the travel agency. The letter informed me that there had been a cancellation and my seat was ready on the plane.

When I boarded that plane I had forty dollars with me and planned to be gone for two weeks. The entire trip was to last a month, but I was only booked for the first half. After the trip to the Holy Land the tour was taking an extended trip to Rome, England, and many other places. I wanted the whole trip.

The suitcase containing my shoes was lost during the flight. So I walked the Holy Land in thongs. Before I knew it, the group with which I was touring presented me with a donation of money to buy some things to wear, and I had money to finish my trip.

One day as we rode the tour bus through the Holy Land, I was sitting on the back seat looking out the window at the desert. All of a sudden we came around a hill and could see into a valley. I stared at it in disbelief. I had been here before. I recognized the terrain. I knew this was where David had killed Goliath.

I yelled to the driver, "Bandy, please stop the bus." There were scheduled stops at particular sightseeing points, but this was not one of them.

He asked, "Ma'am?"

I said again, "Please stop the bus. I want a picture." Everyone looked out the bus windows to see what I wanted a picture of. I said, "Trust me." Bandy stopped the bus and got off with me while the others sat there.

As we stood there, he looked quizzically at me. I asked him, "Is that the hill where the Philistines came against Israel?"

He looked startled. "Why, yes."

"Is this where David came to fight Goliath?"

Again he replied in the affirmative. Then, his

curiosity not to be contained, he asked, "Have you been here before?"

I smiled and answered, "Yes, but I don't think you would understand. I just wanted to take a picture. Let's go." It was awesome to realize I had stood physically in the land where once I had spiritually been in the vision when God taught me about the weapons to use against Goliath.

Though I had learned much from my Teacher, I was soon to discover that I had scarcely begun to learn His ways. There was a change coming for which I was not quite prepared. The place of ministry I was enjoying was all I expected to have. But that was not what the Lord had in mind. Another transition period was about to begin in my life. And, once again, I would have to prove my consecration to my lovely Lord. ∾

Nine

Introduction to
West Coast Ministry
❧

I WAS SEATED BESIDE a pastor from the state of
Washington on our return flight to New York
from the Holy Land. We chatted, and I found that
he was continuing on the trip. I told him I wished I
could go on the rest of the trip.

"Have you prayed about it?" he asked.

I replied, "Well, no."

He said, "Let's pray. Jesus, if You want her to continue on this trip, open the door."

At the place where those traveling for only two
weeks would leave for home while the others continued the trip for another two weeks, an executive
with the group tour boarded the plane and asked
who Fuchsia Parrish was. I raised my hand, and he
came over and said, "We have just had a cancellation for the rest of the trip. A passenger's father

died, and he left his ticket. You may finish the rest of the trip in his place."

I traveled two more weeks and, after a month's trip, came home with more money than what I had when I left.

I had forgotten that the Lord told me He was going to introduce me to the man who would introduce me to the man who would open doors for me on the West Coast. Before I left Atlanta I had heard God tell me that I would go to the West Coast. But I didn't know when.

So I told George that I wanted to go to the West Coast. My friend Thelma Drye and I planned to attend the General Conference of the Assemblies on God in Seattle. We rented a nine-foot trailer and drove all the way from Greensboro, North Carolina, to Seattle, Washington. We planned to be gone a month. While I had been on the trip to the Holy Land, several pastors had told me, "Whenever you are on the West Coast, let me know."

I had taken their names, and Thelma and I had written letters to these pastors informing them of our trip to the West Coast.

As Thelma and I pulled out at two o'clock in the morning for the trip to the West Coast, we dropped our letters in what we thought was a red, white, and blue post office box on a street corner. (At that time, many government properties were painted in red, white, and blue.) It wasn't until much later that we realized we had thrown them into a government trash can painted red, white, and blue.

We arrived at the conference, expecting to meet the ministers to whom we had sent letters. However, after four days at the conference, no one had invited me to preach in their church. I told my coworker that we would start for home when the conference closed. I did not tell her that we didn't have enough money to make the trip home.

As we stood in the foyer the last night of the conference, Dr. Peterson, the chairman of the Assemblies of God, came walking through. (On our trip to the Holy Land, when one of his assistants found out that I was a nurse, he had asked me to write a prescription for medicine to treat Dr. Peterson's poison ivy, and I had gladly done so.) Now, as Dr. Peterson recognized me, he came to greet me and asked, "Sister Parrish, what are you doing here?"

I responded, "Well, I came to hold some meetings, but I haven't seen the pastors who invited me, so we will be going back home tomorrow."

We were about to witness a miracle. The last morning of the conference was reserved for business, and usually nothing was allowed on the agenda except church business. Committee reports lasted about two hours. There was no exception to this policy because of all the business matters that were at hand.

My friend and I were in that last morning meeting. When I walked into the meeting that morning, Brother Peterson walked onto the platform, excused himself to the conference, and said, "I have an announcement to make. There are two lovely young women attending this conference. They are women of God, and God has sent them out here to minister. I hope someone will hear this announcement." Then he asked us to stand, and he introduced us to the conference.

Dr. Judson Cornwall was sitting in the congregation with his wife, Eleanor. Because of his disappointment with previous meetings, he had declared he would not continue to have "revival meetings" in his church—had not had one for five years. After the meeting, this little man with a mustache walked up to me with his wife beside him. After he had introduced himself and his wife, Eleanor, he said to his wife, "This is my next evangelist."

Eleanor said to him, "You said you weren't going to have any more revivals."

Brother Cornwall had never seen me before, but he responded, "I will now."

He asked, "How are you traveling?"

"We are pulling a little trailer," I said.

He replied, "I won't be home until Wednesday, but here is my address and that of my church. Take your trailer to my church and hook it up in the church parking lot. There will be someone there to help you."

He didn't even ask me if I wanted to go. He just said, "We will start our revival on Friday night." We drove that little trailer from Seattle, Washington, to Eugene, Oregon, pulled up in the church yard, parked that little trailer, and waited for Brother and Sister Cornwall to come home. He arrived on Wednesday, as he said, and on Friday evening we began our week of revival meetings.

It was Saturday morning, and I didn't have any money for groceries. I said to Thelma, "We need some things to eat, don't we?"

She said, "Yes, we need some groceries."

I said, "Tell me what we need."

I sat down with a piece of paper to make a

grocery list at the tiny kitchen table. She said, "Well, if we had some rice, we have some things to cook with it." She listed four or five other things and said we could make out with that.

I pressed her, "What else do we need?"

She looked at me questioningly, knowing I didn't have the money. Then she added several other things it would be nice to have. I wrote them down.

I held that piece of paper up in the air and prayed, "All right, Lord, here is the grocery list. I hold it up to You."

That was Saturday morning about eleven o'clock. About twelve noon I went to the church to pray, knowing I had to preach the next day. I did not know the people, and I was quaking with fear inside.

As I entered the church, I met a man and his wife who were cleaning the church. He said, "Are you the minister that was to come to our church?"

I said, "Yes, I am Fuchsia Parrish."

He introduced himself and then said, "My wife thinks I am crazy. We went grocery shopping earlier . . . " He paused as if embarrassed, then said, "I have never done anything like this."

I asked his wife, "What did he do?"

She said, "He got a second grocery cart and told me to go ahead. He said he had a list to get, too. He felt he should share some groceries with the evangelists. These are the things he bought for the minister who is holding the revival."

I looked in the bag; it contained exactly what I had ordered from God. I stood there and double-checked the list. He had given us everything I had ordered.

That answer to prayer started a revival in my own heart. I knew I was where I was supposed to be. I knew the Holy Spirit had released me on the West Coast. I preached for one week and expected to close the meeting. But at the end of the week, Brother Cornwall said to me, "You are not leaving. I want you to stay for another week."

I preached as I had first begun, sharing the fresh revelation that God had shown me that day. It was during this meeting that I preached my first sermon, "The Seven Moods of the Holy Spirit."[1] Brother Cornwall sat and listened intently.

Suddenly, he jumped up in the middle of my message and stomped his foot. It was strange to see this dignified college music professor acting this way in front of his congregation. I thought he must have seen a black spider or something. I tried to ignore him and went on preaching. He turned around and sat back down.

When I finished preaching, he came up to the platform and said, "In this service tonight I have stomped my ambitions—my desire to be a part of the higher order and to go to headquarters. I experienced this kind of preaching and revelation years ago, and I am not going to leave it now for position."

He has testified many times that God really met him personally during those meetings.

The next morning as Pastor Judson Cornwall walked out of his house the Holy Spirit spoke to him, "Judson, Fuchsia Parrish is your sister. Take care of her. I want her to minister on the West Coast."

When he came to see me, his first words to me were, "I guess you and I better get to know each other. You are my sister." He told me that God had told him to take care of me. He offered his office and church as our base of ministry.

REVELATION OF ESTHER

REVELATION OF THE WORD through supernatural visitations of God in my life continued during this time. Not only was the Holy Spirit shining His wonderful light on the written Word, giving me understanding that I had not had before, but I received revelation through visions that opened realities of His Word to me.

One evening while I was in Brother Cornwall's church's prayer room, God took me out in the Spirit and taught me the Book of Esther. Dr. Cornwall sat on a prayer bench in the room and took notes. He heard me talking to God. I was talking my side of the book. When I returned to my natural senses in the early hours of the morning, he and Thelma were sitting with me. He complained, "This is not fair. I only heard one side of the conversation. Go home and write the rest of it. While it is still fresh, I want it. It will fade if you don't record it."

That was the night God said to me, "I have brought you to the kingdom for such a time as this." I did write the vision, and it has since been published in my book, *For Such a Time As This*.

In the vision I was transported into the palace of Esther. I went to the geographical setting of the Book of Esther. And I understood that this was more than a historical event. It was a prophetic allegory. I saw the church. I saw the bride.

I began to realize what happened to Esther when she went through the preparation of the harem experience. She was willing to submit to a period of purification with many spices, each representing a special work of the Spirit. Before she became his bride, she was trained in the manners of the palace to behave in ways that please the king. Her experience parallels that of every believer who desires an intimate relationship with the Lord Jesus and is willing to be molded into the image of Christ.

I saw the work of Mordecai, a type of the Holy Spirit. As I watched Mordecai's vigilence over Esther, I understood that this allegory teaches us how the Holy Spirit walks in our temples, coming to all fifteen of our spiritual gates every day in order to protect us and to prepare us for our relationship with the King.

I saw Haman as a type of the flesh and realized how subtle he was. As I lay there on the floor in a trance, I asked questions while the whole book was being revealed to me. I asked, "What was Haman symbolic of?"

The Spirit showed me that Haman is a type of the flesh. At the time, I didn't know that the Cornwalls were listening. I was just carrying on a conversation with my Teacher.

I saw the battle with Haman in the royal court. I saw how Haman tried to kill Mordecai. And I understood that our flesh would do the same damage to the work of the Holy Spirit in us and in the church. I saw that the enemy was going to try to destroy the church. I was struck by the hatred that Haman had for Mordecai and by Mordecai's devotion to Esther as he walked in the gates to see how she was doing.

I saw that Esther communicated with Mordecai, giving him reports of what was happening in her life. And Mordecai warned Esther and gave her instructions about what she must do to try to save her people. It was so beautiful to me that Mordecai stayed near the palace all night and put on sackcloth to pray and intercede for Esther and for his people.

When Esther prepared a banquet for the king, I understood that was a type of the worship of the church and that the church would win the victory over the flesh and the enemy in worship. Esther did not ask for anything. She went in first to invite the king to her banquet. On three subsequent occasions she didn't say a word to the king to ask him about saving her life—she simply prepared a place of worship.

I understood that we would be brought into the presence of the King, and then we could tell our hearts' desire in His presence. I saw that the church was going to win the victory in worship.

The whole analogy opened to me.

Esther's greatest desire was to commune together at the banquet table with the king. I was thrilled to understand that she wanted Haman to come. She knew that there was no place on earth where Haman could be overcome except in the presence of the king. Allegorically, I saw that we have to take our flesh with us into the presence of the King. That is where the flesh will be dealt with. The flesh is handled effectively in worship. Isaiah understood this when he had his throne-conscious experience and cried out:

> Woe is me! for I am undone; because I am a man of unclean lips, and I dwell in the midst of a people of unclean lips: for mine eyes have seen the King, the LORD of hosts. Then

flew one of the seraphims unto me, having a live coal in his hand, which he had taken with the tongs from off the altar: and he laid it upon my mouth, and said, Lo, this hath touched thy lips; and thne iniquity is taken away, and thy sin purged.

—ISAIAH 6:5–7

I saw that when Esther went in the last time, she asked for her life and the life of her people. God spoke to me as clearly as I have ever heard Him in my life: "Unless you who carry the Word are 'lifed,' you and My people will die. There is nothing that will save the people of God except My divine life. If you are not pregnant with My life, you cannot 'life' the people with the living, incorruptible Word (seed) of God."

I saw the church dying because of programs and man's structure that had no life in it.

I saw Esther standing in the presence of the king, and the Lord said to me that night, "Daughter, you are as Esther. I want you to take life to My people. I have brought you to the kingdom for such a time as this."

I knew from that night on I was to be "lifed" with the Word or I would not be able to minister the eternal Word of God to the people. Before I go to the pulpit, I pray every time, "Life me and life the people."

I saw the church dying for lack of revelation and life in the Word. There is no merit in sharing information from the Word or opinions or good ideas. It is the seed of the living Word that must be imparted to our hearts so that we can live in Him.

A Cross Is Hung

MY HUSBAND, GEORGE, and I both were assured I had moved in the will of God by traveling to those meetings on the West Coast. We were agreed that we would like to move to the state of Oregon. He especially looked forward to fishing in the Rogue River for recreation, for he was an ardent fisherman. He anticipated resigning from his work, and we were discussing our plans for our future on the West Coast. I made preparations to return home to North Carolina to complete our dream plans to return with my husband and minister on the West Coast. As Thelma and I drove back to North Carolina, I was excited about the future.

Yet, there was a slight premonition in my heart that competed for recognition with the excitement I was feeling. For nearly one year God had been impressing on me that I was to take my "Isaac" to Mount Moriah. In conversation with my husband, I learned that God had shared the same challenge with him. Both of us knew we had to be willing to sacrifice our Isaac, and we did not know if we would bring "him" back down the mountain as Abraham did.

One day while talking to someone on the phone, I was doodling on a piece of paper (very un-characteristic of me). When I hung up the phone, I realized I had drawn a cross and underneath it wrote the words, "A cross is hung," along with a time—3:00 A.M. There was a soberness in that moment that pierced my heart.

George had previously been admitted to the hos-pital for what we thought would be a simple

111

surgery for hernia, a repair from a previous service-related injury. But shortly after I returned home to North Carolina, George slipped off to be with Jesus one night while he was asleep—3:00 A.M. I knew that I had gone to Mount Moriah, and I did not get to bring my Isaac back down the mountain as Abraham did. Indeed, a cross was hung in my life.

One month after all my business matters were settled, I broke up our household, gave away the furniture, and bought a larger trailer. Once again, Thelma Drye and I started the long trip to the West Coast. There I would begin a new phase of life—without George—in a ministry that I had not yet known.

It was then that Thelma Drye, my traveling companion, became my coworker. She was a tremendous prayer warrior and carried the prayer ministry in every church where we went to hold services. She met with people of the church to pray for me and for the work of God in that place. Only eternity will reveal the powerful effect that prayer support had on our ministry together.

When we arrived in Oregon, the Cornwalls again supported and watched over us in a close relationship as a protective brother and sister in the Lord. Dr. Cornwall began scheduling meetings for me, and God blessed our meetings tremendously. In revival after revival throughtout the states of Oregon, Washington, and into the borders of Canada, we saw God change lives and bring His healing power to many. ∾

Ten

Revival and Revelation

I N MANY OF the churches that invited me for a week of meetings, God worked so mightily that the meetings were extended up to eight weeks. Dr. Cornwall would have to call the next church on the schedule, saying he was sorry, but God was moving powerfully and the meetings were continuing where I was.

For the next six years Thelma and I traveled up and down the West Coast ministering continually and seeing God move in healing and revival wherever we went. During those years of continuous traveling ministry on the West Coast, I can truly say I felt deeply loved. That was when I first heard people say, "You look and sound like Ma Beall."

I asked who she was. They seemed surprised and asked, "You don't know Ma Beall?"

I later learned that she was the founder and pastor of Bethesda Missionary Temple in Detroit, Michigan. Her three-thousand-seat "armory" became a center for the Latter Rain movement, attracting thousands of visitors who were seeking a fresh anointing from God.[1] Judson Cornwall and his wife, Eleanor, even remarked that I reminded them of her.

Others asked me if I knew Aimee Semple McPherson. I had to answer that I did not. Nor had I heard of Smith Wigglesworth and other powerful ministries that people had witnessed. I came out of a Methodist background. I knew nothing about others who had ministered before me in the power of the Holy Spirit. I felt as if I had been ushered into another world of people with powerful ministries that I did not know existed.

REVELATION OF THE HYDROELECTRIC POWER PLANT

AFTER WE HAD gone back to the West Coast, holding meetings for several months, I went to Klamath Falls, Oregon, for a meeting. I was scheduled for one week of meetings there. However, the meetings were extended for eight weeks because of the wonderful move of God we were experiencing.

I had been recently widowed, and one Sunday evening as I watched the people leaving the church to go to their homes, I prepared to go back to the home where Thelma and I were staying. I had turned back to the pulpit to get my Bible when I heard the Holy Spirit say to me, "Spend the night with Me. I have something to show you."

So I went to the pastor and asked if I could spend the night at the church. On the West Coast it was customary to have special meetings on every night except Monday night. I knew there would be no meeting the next evening. The pastor was quick to give me permission to stay, and he assured me that it was safe to do so.

I sat down on the platform and waited for the Lord to show me something. He spoke to me, saying, "I want to show you what is going to happen in the church world before Jesus returns for the bride. I want to show you how I will pour out My Spirit upon all flesh."

I had been very influenced by the teaching that the church was just going to slip out some night in the Rapture when Christ returned. I was not aware that God intended to pour out revival on the earth before the second return of Christ. As I sat there on the platform over the next several hours, the Holy Spirit opened my eyes to see a vision of the building of a hydroelectric power plant in the earth. This vision made such an impression on me that I know I cannot adequately express it.[2]

I watched a crew dig a deep foundation. I did not understand what I was seeing, but I knew He was showing me something profound. I saw a deep excavation.

I saw how meticulous God was with the construction of the foundation of that power plant. The sand had to be just right; the soil had to be just right. The foundation of that power plant was very important. It was not prepared in a few minutes. It was built by a skilled crew who knew exactly how to lay the foundation. Then I watched them as they erected the power plant. It was huge with many mammoth gates.

HISTORICAL STREAMS OF TRUTH

I UNDERSTOOD THAT the water that would fill this great plant was the Word of God and that the power plant was the church. God showed me that the water of the Word left the throne of God and came down through time from the beginning of the church.

I saw streams that represented all the great revelators—Martin Luther, John Knox, John Wesley—and others who were responsible for entire movements, denominations, and doctrinal positions. I saw streams of truth that had left the throne, been dammed up, and the water had stopped running.

As I watched the crew build, the Lord began to talk to me about the river of God that had brought streams of truth to the church throughout history. He showed me how the pure water of truth had filled the church as it came from the throne of God, but that it had been dammed up. The river wasn't running as a river now but as tiny streams that appeared as dribbles coming out of the gates.

The stream of *regeneration* was there—"The just shall live by his faith" (Hab. 2:4)—flowing back to the church in the Dark Ages through Martin Luther. It brought wonderful reformation to the church but was later dammed up in Lutheranism.

Then I saw the truth of *holiness* leave the throne and flow to the church through John Wesley. It was dammed up and became the extreme of legalism to many.

The wonderful truth of *predestination* flowed down through the Episcopal and Presbyterian churches, giving light about the eternal plan of God. But it was dammed up as the doctrine of predetermined election that condemned men to hell involuntarily.

The truth of the *security* of the believer flowed into the church but was dammed up into unconditional security. At first it had balanced the truth brought by John Wesley that urged self-effort in practicing a holy life. But it was taken to the once-saved-always-saved extreme by many.

I saw that many redeeming truths that left the river of God as streams to be embraced by the church had been contaminated by man's interpretation that dammed them up into error. However, the seed truth was still there. The End-Time revival that God is soon sending is a river of truth that will wash away the error and purify the church to bring faith, holiness, the eternal plan of God, and the security of the believer into perfect balance.

Every truth that has left the throne has been dammed up by prejudice, tradition, denominationalism, culture, and custom. I saw that God was going to rectify that in His church.

MY WORD WILL NOT RETURN VOID

THE HOLY SPIRIT brought to my mind Isaiah 55:11: "My word . . . shall not return unto me void." Then He asked me, "Would you like to know what I meant when I said that?"

My first thought was, *I guess I must not have it right, or You wouldn't be asking me if I would like to know what it meant.* "Yes," I responded.

"Where was the Word to begin with?"

"At the throne."

"I sent the Word," He explained. "And Christ is

now seated at My throne, but the Word hasn't yet come back."

My understanding was opened to the Scripture that describes the kenosis of Jesus when He emptied Himself to become man and a servant of men; then He suffered death, even the death of the cross. (See Philippians 2.) He is the Word according to the Gospel of John (John 1:1). And He will not return "empty" or "void" into the presence of the Father.

While we understand that Christ is the living Word, the Bible also teaches that believers are to be known as living epistles read and known of all men (2 Cor. 3:2–3). The Word of God is to be written on tablets of flesh—in the hearts of all born-again believers. And Christ will bring many sons to glory, of whom He is the firstfruits. In that way the Word will not return void—empty. As sons and daughters of God, we will go back home in Christ the Word.

The prayer Jesus prayed in the garden was to bring us back with the glory that He had with the Father before the beginning—that we could be in Him as He is in the Father. There is a profound reality here that I had never understood in my interpretation of "the Word will not return void."

I had taught that preaching the Word would bring good results; it would not return void of impact. And the Holy Spirit did not take away that possibility of interpretation. But He impressed me with the true reality that the Word of God, Christ Himself, is not going to return "empty" to the Father. We are going home in Him as living epistles.

Now I am seeing that all the truths of God that left the throne have come down to the church as streams—every major doctrine has been received by the church and then dammed up and interpreted by man. Denominations were formed according to the "CODE"—the Pharisaical interpretations of men that have divided the body of Christ and insisted they alone had the true "divine order."

The streams of truth in the church today are more voluminous than ever before in church history. And the coming revival, the move of God that I saw represented in the analogy of the hydroelectric plant, is going to unlock the gates. The flood is going to cleanse the church. It is not going to have just a few truths in it. It is going to reveal the Word as it was when it left the throne—in purity—and it will be for healing for the nations.

In the vision God gave me He was building a new power plant, and this time it was going to be able to carry the water. The Holy Spirit spoke to me, "This time when I turn the switch, no devil, no demon, no man, or no denomination will ever be able to dam it up again."

The church is going to become the glorious church without spot or wrinkle that God intended her to become.

I did not understand the technical workings of a power plant when I received the vision. But as I began to tell others what I had experienced, I described tubular screens that were put in the gates to be sure that the water was kept clean and sifted. I used other technical terms that were later validated by engineers who declared my description to be scientifically correct.

That night I watched in my vision as the power plant was constructed layer upon layer and gate upon gate. Then I saw Jesus take that power plant in His hands. I saw Jesus as a huge person towering over the gigantic power plant. When He held it in His hands, I asked, "Where is it going?"

He took me down to a church where He had turned the power loose. It was a nondescript church building with no outside framework. I saw the pulpit; I saw a minister. And I saw the power being channeled through the church. God let me know that the river would come through preaching of the Word. He is the river. His power must be turned loose to flood over the dams that were blocking the flow of God's Word—allowing the streams of truth to flow freely once again.

As the Word came down through the church, I saw that there were no sides to the church. I understood that it was the church universal. Then I saw the river run out from that church and flow in several directions. Beneath the water I saw a harvest field covering the earth.

As the river ran to churches, I saw five geographical points in the United States where those waters were channeled into great transformers. One of them on the West Coast had a shadow over it. It seemed the power had been released there before, and something had blocked it. It would have to be cleared. Another transformer was in New York. There was one in the Midwest, one in the lower central part of the states, and one in Florida. Then I saw the water flow out of the United States, but before it did, it was channeled into underground pipes.

God was getting ready to turn the water loose. I saw churches as reservoirs and cisterns. Then the Spirit spoke to me and said, "Watch Me."

As I watched, He ran underground pipes and

connected the churches to the power from the transformers in each geographical location. I understood there would not just be one place from where God distributed His power. There are some geographical points where His power is going to break forth as hubs, but His power also will be channeled to networking churches that have been prepared to receive the Word of God. Local churches will be full of the water—just like cisterns. Many of these churches seemed to think they were experiencing this move of God by themselves. They didn't know they were part of a network or dynamo. But they were filled with the life-giving water of the Word.

My heart broke as I watched God pass by church after church that was not ready to receive the water of the Word. And when He encountered individual cisterns, He ran underground pipes where no one saw them, networking the cisterns to the river. He turned to me and said, "When I get them all hooked up, I will pull the switch."

He intended to let the river run into all the reservoirs and cisterns—places that had been dug out with hunger for the Word, purity of heart, and by seeking God for His presence.

In 1963, when I saw this networking of churches in the vision—connecting them together with underground pipes—there was no such thing as ministers and churches working together. Thirty-five years ago this was a foreign concept—even within denominations. There was not even an awareness of each other. Today the term *networking* is used freely to describe the unity of pastors working and praying together, seeking God for His supernatural harvest.

There were no "concerts of prayer" in cities

Many times the fact was that preachers didn't speak to each other. More recently we are reading about the concept of a concert of prayer that encircles the world. Such prayer is part of the vision I received in 1963. I saw ministers and churches networking together through that analogy of the power plant and its underground pipes.

END-TIME HARVEST

UNDERNEATH THIS MAMMOTH power plant I saw a harvest field stretching throughout the world. It was golden and ready for harvest. The wheat was ripe and bending its head over in great heaviness. As I watched, the water began to be released, and I heard the song, "It Is Harvest Time."

After I viewed the whole process of building and connecting the power plant, He took me back to look at the main plant. It was empty! The water had not been turned loose. As He was preparing to turn loose the water, He took me to the top of the power plant. There I saw something that resembled an old Victrola speaker, from which I heard four songs.

The first song I heard was "Jesus Saves." When I heard it, I said to God, "That is an old hymn." I thought that this new thing I was seeing shouldn't involve something old like this hymn. But as I listened to it, I understood that the revival was going to bring great salvation. He impressed me that I had never seen or heard of such salvations as we were going to see.

The second song I heard was "Where the Healing Waters Flow." I didn't know that song very well, but He said to me, "When I begin to turn the waters loose, there won't be just physical healing. When this water is released there will be full salvation like you have never seen. There will be healing for body, soul, and spirit. I will heal My church. She will not come home with scars. My healing water is not going to heal just physical diseases and bones; it is going to heal every trace of disease in mind, emotions, and spirit as well."

I remembered the verse in Isaiah: "He was wounded for our transgressions, he was bruised for our iniquities: the chastisement of our peace was upon him" (Isa. 53:5).

The third hymn I heard was "It's a Glorious Church Without Spot or Wrinkle." I could hear the words to the verse, "Don't you hear them coming, Brother, Coming o'er the hills of time." And I could hear the church marching in step, the music bringing them nearer. I knew He would bring together a clean and glorious church.

Then the fourth song I heard was the chorus "The Earth Shall Be Filled With the Knowledge of the Glory of the Lord." Though I have taught about the glory, and written about it, I have only glimpsed what the glory really is. The Scripture talks about the "knowledge of the glory of the LORD" covering the earth. The revelation knowledge of the glory of God will cover the earth as the waters cover the sea. (See Habakkuk 2:14.)

When I heard that song, the Lord said to me, "My church must be delivered from prejudice, de-nominationalism, culture, custom, and tradition." It was then that He said, "And this time, when I pull the switch to open the gates and let the river flow, no demon, no devil, no man, and no denomination will ever dam it up again."

Sunday night had passed, and most of Monday as well, before the vision of the power plant stopped rolling before me. I left the church on Monday afternoon and went home to write the vision and draw what I could and interpret it. I didn't finish it until Tuesday. We called an engineer, Brother McGuire, to look at the drawing and read the notes about it. When he read it, he cried like a baby—knowing I could not understand technically what I had drawn.

He decided to take it to a power company in Portland, Oregon. I had written words down that I did not understand. I just wrote what the Spirit told me. (I would give anything if I still had a copy of what I wrote.) The engineer asked the people at the plant if they would critique a transcript for him, saying, "It is very important to us that we understand this material and know whether or not it is correct. The person who wrote it is deeply concerned as to its accuracy. If you would not mind taking some time to critique it, we would greatly appreciate it." They agreed to do so.

When my host returned to the power company a few days later, the president of the company wanted to see him. A receptionist ushered him into the office of the president. After greeting him kindly, the president asked, "Where did you get this information?"

My host responded, "What would you say if I told you that a little woman who cannot fix a light switch wrote it?"

"I would say she is pulling your leg," the president retorted. "This paper is one of the most scientific papers I have ever read. There are words and terms in her paper that only a few master electricians know and understand. Whoever wrote this paper is a master electrician."

"Please forgive me," my host responded. "I should not have said it was a little lady who wrote it; she just copied it down. The Master Electrician—the Holy Spirit—described it to her."

When I began to preach what I had seen, people looked at me as if I had lost my marbles. Much of the church at that time was living with a defeatist mentality, filled with unbelief, expecting things to get worse and worse, and looking forward to escaping some night in the Rapture. When I began to preach the great revival that was coming, the networking and filling up of the reservoirs with the water of the Word, many people were incredulous. Up and down the West Coast I preached that God was going to send a great End-Time revival that would bring in a wonderful harvest of souls. My preaching went against the grain of much of the theology of the day.

Now when I stand up in churches and say we are living in the greatest hour in church history, it is because the truth is more voluminous than it has ever been—the gates are open, and the water is running. And the knowledge of the glory of the Lord is going to cover the earth.

EZEKIEL'S RIVER

AFTER RECEIVING THIS vision, the Spirit opened to me the Book of Ezekiel where Ezekiel saw the waters being measured. (See Ezekiel 47.) He showed me the river, and I began to understand what the levels of the water involved. The first measure was to the *ankles.* That was symbolic of the first thousand years—from Abraham to David—when the water of the Word ran ankle-deep. During that time God revealed Himself as the covenant God to His people.

The second measure was knee-deep, representing the second thousand years from David to Christ. During this period God gave David the revelation of the tabernacle and the temple of worship. Christ, the living Word, revealed the Father to us.

Then, except for the bright years of the early church from the time of Christ's ascension until A.D. 1500, the church suffered the loss of revelation during the subsequent Dark Ages and until the time of the Reformation.

The last measure Ezekiel saw was water deep enough to swim in. From the time of the Reformation to now the water level has been rising and gaining momentum. The water Ezekiel saw was filled with fish, foretelling the harvest that is coming. And, in Ezekiel's vision, the waters were for the healing of the nations.

The great revival that is coming is not going to miss America. But it is flowing all over the world. The waters of the hydroelectric power plant ran from America to the isles of the sea. Recently, as I sat on the board of regents in the Bahamas with the representatives of twenty-seven nations, I felt the awe of God. It was awesome to see these Christian leaders from the isles of the sea and other Third World nations networking and fellowshiping together.

Since that vision thirty years ago, I have been to many churches in America where I have heard the sound of those waters, confirming that they are reservoirs that are now being connected to the network of pipes. In churches on the isles of Trinidad, the Bahamas, Hawaii, and in the nations of South America, I have heard those supernatural waters running. I'm sure they are running in places I have not been as well. God's truth is being stored up, the water levels are rising, and God is getting ready to release His power in the earth in real Holy Ghost revival to bring in the harvest. ∽

Eleven

A New Name

I HAD BEEN ENJOYING wonderful ministry on the West Coast for six years, but now the Lord had other plans for me. At first, I could not see clearly His plans. It took me six months to submit my will to His will; I keenly understood that to do what He was asking meant that I had to lose my identity—surrender my ministry completely to Him who had been so fruitful and satisfying to me.

The leader of a large ministry in Dallas flew out to the West Coast and asked me to please come and join his ministry. He told me that it was God's will for me, and he wanted me to be dean of his Bible college as well as a conference evangelist. We seemed to share the same vision, and, as a widow, I was made to believe that it was right for me to submit to the leadership of a man. This minister had the vision I had for training men and women to go to the nations and bring in the revival I had seen in the vision of the hydroelectric power plant.

Many of my friends with whom I had ministered on the West Coast for the past six years did not understand why I would consider leaving such a fruitful ministry while it was at its peak. But I felt I had heard God's call for change, and I answered it. After six months of deliberation with God, I joined the vision of a man who I felt had the same burden as I did—and the finances to support it. The Lord asked me if I was willing to lose my identity. I literally expected to go into the situation and never be heard of again. I thought I would put my shoulders to the work of someone who had my vision for revival and lay my life down for it.

I enjoyed the work there with the students. The schools grew quickly to over one thousand students, many of whom were going to the mission field. The Lord taught me a lot of lessons there. And the Lord had another surprise for me there, one that I did not expect.

A SPECIAL STUDENT

THE LEADER OF the work asked me if I would teach a Bible class one morning a week to the entire staff of the complex, including the faculty of all the schools, the printshop and cafeteria workers, and other auxiliary staff. I agreed to teach the class. At the beginning of that class, I asked the new staff members and teachers to stand and introduce themselves. Among those who stood was a handsome man who said, "My name is Leroy Pickett. I am head of the sound engineering department."

I greeted him cordially, "We are delighted to have you, Mr. Pickett."

Little did I dream that God had sent that man to that college to become an integral part of my life and ministry.

Leroy was a single man, having recently left the Air Force after seven years of service. He had given his life to the Lord and come to work at the college where I was teaching. He had never married, and I had been a widow for several years. Because I had no one to go home to care for, I often stayed in my office until the wee hours of the morning, studying, researching, and helping other teachers. Leroy had an apartment at the college and would come by my office to see if I was all right and if I wanted anything to eat or drink. Quite often I would say *yes,* and he would bring me something for dinner. He would check the doors at night. I thought he was kind to look out for me.

I discovered that he was "Mr. Fix-it." He could fix anything that was broken. I began to bring things from home—broken necklaces and other things— for him to repair.

Later he teased me about "chasing" him. I looked at him in amazement and asked, "How can you say I chased you?"

He replied, "You broke everything you had and asked me to fix it."

I had to admit there was some truth to that. But however it happened, we became wonderful friends, and for several years I insisted that we were only friends. But finally I began to realize that he was coming by my office more and more and seemed more protective of me, and our relationship grew into more than friendship.

Some time later we were married in the chapel at the college. My dear friend became my husband who has worked with me so faithfully in the ministry. Leroy is known to my audiences as "my honey" and has become more dear to me through these last years of ministry. As we have traveled together constantly, we have grown closer than ever in our relationship.

We had a wonderful honeymoon given to us—a trip to New York to enjoy all the tourist events there. Coming home from New York, we discussed going to the mission field together. At that time we felt we were part of a wonderful ministry that was reaching many states and countries. But not long after that, Leroy walked into my office and said, "Honey, I am leaving the work here. I am going to look for a job in the community. I am not telling you what to do, but this ministry has not remained clean. It is going to fall."

I was dean of the college then. I decided to stay for the rest of the semester and graduate that class. The day after we handed out the diplomas, there was a big board meeting of the college. The Holy Spirit revealed to me that I was leaving, and I handed in my resignation. It was one of the hardest things I ever did. The response of the board was very difficult for me. I was accused of laying down the cross and backsliding, losing out on my place in the bride. It was a painful time for my husband and me, and we did not know where to go.

Before long, people began to knock on the door of our home, asking if I would be willing to teach them. Then doors opened to teach Bible classes in homes in other cities. We started having Bible classes in our living room.

As the classes grew, the people asked me to become their pastor. The Holy Spirit had taught me about Christ dwelling in His church. But I felt I did not understand how to apply all the new truths in the practical running of a local church. As I prayed for wisdom, I heard Him say, "Faithful is He that hath you, for He will do it."

Then He answered me with one sentence: "Take care of that to which the Word gravitates."

Running water follows a course that is open to it. I understood that I was to go open a river, build a fountain, get a place ready for the water, and then take care of everything to which the Word gravitates.

I didn't sit down and draw designs for a church building and facilities. I started teaching the Word in a Bible class. As the class grew in numbers, we secured a large meeting room in the Modern America building. As parents brought their children, I realized we needed to meet the needs of the children. One of our families, the John Wests, had a large garage, and we turned it into an academy for the children that God gave us. We were building a church to which the Word could gravitate. We were digging a reservoir for the Word.

We first called the church Christian Word Ministries. When young people came who wanted training in the Word, we began our Bible college with a four-year curriculum of classes. We felt impressed of the Lord to call the Bible school "Fountaingate," expressing the understanding that living waters would flow into us and out from us as we trained and sent students into ministry. We did not realize at the time that we would see those waters go to the ends of the earth as former students of the Bible college ministered in many nations. I thought we were building a local church, but the Lord removed that idea—the vision was bigger than that. He simply instructed us to take care of everything to which the Word gravitated. We became known as Fountaingate Ministries.

As the church continued to grow, we tried to meet the needs of the people who gravitated to the Word. Doors opened for radio and television ministries, and we developed a tape-lending library, many videos for weekly Bible college classes in other citites, as well as a little lambs' school and other outreach ministries. Wherever the water ran, we tried to reap the harvest. God brought a host of precious people to help—as well as faithful staff members: Dr. Judson Cornwall, Dr. Charlotte Baker, and other ministers to assist in the ministry. He allowed us to minister to so many precious people and to share some of these visions with them. They have become a part of it.

REVELATION OF THE JOSHUA GENERATION

DURING THE SEVENTEEN years we pastored Fountaingate Ministries, God continued to reveal His Word to me—sometimes through visions and conversations with my Teacher. He deepened our revelation of worship and let us enjoy some of the most wonderful worship services in His presence that I have known. I was honored to be chosen as one of the deans of the International Worship Symposium. These conferences brought churches and leaders throughout the country, flowing in and through the Charismatic Renewal, into a greater expression of corporate worship.

There was also a wonderful movement among the youth of our nation during these years, and God prepared me to minister to large numbers of them on several occasions by giving me a wonderful revelation of His intent for the present-day Joshua generation.

As I was waiting on God for a message to the graduating class of Fountaingate Bible College, I asked Him for a message that would change their lives and let them know God had spoken to them.[1]

As I waited for God to respond to my request for a message, my Father asked me to talk to Him about the wilderness through which Moses led the children of Israel. He wanted me to describe the people I saw in the wilderness. I tried to recall everything I had ever learned about the people in the wilderness and proceeded to describe them. They were people who marched out of Egypt under the leadership and sovereignty of the almighty, omnipotent, omniscient, and omnipresent God. Before going very far, however, they desired to go back to Egypt. They were murmurers, complainers, and faultfinders who rebelled against the sovereign ways that God visited His people to meet their needs. They built the golden calf, refused to believe the voice of the prophets, and died in that wilderness.

After I finished my dismal description of those wilderness people, my Father said He wanted to talk to me about the wilderness in which I was living. He spoke to me concerning the economic status of our country, the political structure, the corruption in our government, and the religious world that is full of apathy and love for materialism. He spoke of the moral status of this wilderness with its promiscuous sex, the curse of AIDS, and the sin of abortion. He gave me a panoramic view of things that are happening in the wilderness of our nation.

Then He said, "On two occasions in history I have invaded this world with a deliverer. The first time I invaded the world in answer to My people's cry and sent Moses to deliver them from Egypt. When Moses was born, the Egyptians were killing the male babies. The second time I invaded this world I sent My Son to deliver My people out of darkness. At the time of Jesus' birth there was also a decree to kill the male babies. Both times Satan thought he had killed My deliverers. My daughter, I am about to invade the world again, and they are killing babies again. But they are not going to destroy My deliverer, for He is the head of the church, and My plan cannot be thwarted."

When my Father had thoroughly established in my thinking the wilderness in which I was living, He focused my attention again on that historical wilderness, asking me if all I saw in that wilderness were the murmurers, complainers, and faultfinders. Then He began to describe another generation that was in that wilderness, one that had been born to the murmurers and complainers, trained by the wilderness testings to depend on God. They knew what it meant to have fresh bread every morning from the Father's hand, and they drank water from the rock. They didn't bow to idols, and they were clothed and fed by God, depending on Him for all their needs.

My Father instructed me to think about the

Joshua generation that had conquered the giants of the Promised Land. "That Joshua generation is alive in your wilderness today," He said, "and they will receive their inheritance and have a part in fulfilling My eternal plan."

I listened intently to what He was saying. It was as though I had never seen that new generation before. The Father declared to me that He was getting ready to take this Joshua generation into the land.

We are living in the most exciting time this world has ever known. Our generation has seen the faithfulness and power of the omnipotent, triune God in the middle of this present wilderness, sustaining such a vast number by supplying them daily bread and giving them to drink from the Rock. I can tell young people that they are living in the greatest hour that has ever been known in church history. They are going to help take this new generation into possessing the inheritance.

Earnestly wanting to understand what He was showing me, I asked my Father, "What is the inheritance?" I told Him that I had heard some people refer to the land of Canaan as a "building program" for their church. They call the new facilities their "Canaan." Others refer to the inheritance of the Promised Land as the victorious, Spirit-filled life. It is true that as individuals we must live holy lives, conquering the "ites" of our self-lives, possessing the land through our obedience. However, that is not the full meaning of receiving our inheritance.

Many of our songs and hymns depict Canaan as heaven, the final destination for weary pilgrims. But Canaan cannot represent heaven, for there are neither giants to conquer in heaven nor battles to win in the presence of the throne of God. I felt I needed a clearer understanding of the reality of the inheritance God had promised to give the Joshua generation of today.

In answer to my question, my Father asked me to go back with Him into the eons of eternity, before time began, and witness the covenant made in the Godhead that was designed to bring to pass their desire for a family. That covenant is the mystery revealed to Paul and is to be fulfilled by the church, the body of Christ. Paul declared: "Christ also loved the church, and gave himself for it; that he might sanctify and cleanse it with the washing of water by the word, that he might present it to himself a glorious church, not having spot, or wrinkle, or any such thing; but that it should be holy and without blemish" (Eph. 5:25–27).

Paul taught that Christ is the head of the church (Eph. 5:23). He also taught that God gave the five-fold ministry to the church for the perfecting of the saints, for the edifying of the body of Christ, "till we all come in the unity of the faith, and of the knowledge of the Son of God, unto a perfect man, unto the measure of the stature of the fulness of Christ" (Eph. 4:13). As unfathomable as it may seem, the Father is going to have such a family in the church who will bear His image.

The inheritance that was partially received in Joshua's generation serves as a type of the promise that is going to be fulfilled in reality in this new generation. The time came when God took Moses home and told Joshua He wanted him to take the generation that He had been training in the wilderness into Canaan. The Scriptures present Joshua as a humble man who had no personal goals other than to please God. He dealt with sin immediately and with finality, and for every successful battle he gave God the glory. He was resourceful in courage, strong in faith, and wholeheartedly committed to God and His law. As a leader he showed the way without fear, conquering the land and dividing the inheritance. God is still calling men and women today whose hearts are like Joshua's.

There were some arduous tasks assigned to Joshua, some that many of us would not have wanted. It was time for the children of Israel to begin to receive their inheritance if they were willing. They were being confronted with the decision: Are you willing to go into the Promised Land? According to the Book of Numbers we find that the first generation as a whole decided they didn't want to go into the land God had promised them. As a result, they wandered for thirty-nine years and died in the wilderness. They were those who had come out of Egypt but were overcome by the "system" of the wilderness. They do not represent sinners, for they had come out of Egypt to follow God. But they refused to go into the Promised Land, and they died in that wilderness.

There are some in the church today who are being overcome by the system of the world, worshiping golden calves, rebelling, and taking part in gossip, criticism, church splits, murmuring, and faultfinding. They do not really know their God. They know *about* Him, but they have no intimate relationship with Him. Though they will not return to Egypt, they will surely perish in the wilderness.

There are others like Michal, King David's wife,

who mocked David when he worshiped hilariously. She was struck with barrenness, the worst curse that could come to a Jewish woman.

There are those like the elder son in the backyard of the prodigal's home, who was a murmurer and complainer and did not join the celebration. He was at the father's house, but he did not rejoice with the father at the return of his prodigal son.

The first generation of Israelites who left Egypt had died without receiving their inheritance, and now God was preparing to take their sons and daughters into the Promised Land. Scripture is very clear regarding our responsibility as part of the Joshua generation who want to enter into our inheritance:

> Every place that the sole of your foot shall tread upon, that have I given unto you . . . There shall not any man be able to stand before thee all the days of thy life: as I was with Moses, so I will be with thee: I will not fail thee, nor forsake thee . . . This book of the law shall not depart out of thy mouth; but thou shalt meditate therein day and night, that thou mayest observe to do according to all that is written therein: for then thou shalt make thy way prosperous, and then thou shalt have good success.
> —JOSHUA 1:3, 5, 8

Before the people of the new generation were ready to receive their inheritance, they had to be tested by life in the wilderness. God is training the church through testings today. Some have taught that the saints aren't supposed to have trials and testings, but testings are necessary to reveal our lack of character and bring us to the place where we can receive His character. God doesn't test us to find out who we are, for He already knows that. *We* don't know who we are until God takes us through the testings and we see our response. The wilderness we are in is God's classroom. When it looks bleak and hopeless we may be tempted to think that God doesn't love us. To the contrary—He loves us so much He is bringing us to spiritual maturity so that we can receive our inheritance. He enables us to look for leaders and to help them train and bring this new generation into their inheritance—the revival that will produce the harvest.

As we have seen, "Canaan" does not refer to heaven, for there are no giants or enemies in heaven. The enemies inside us are the "ites" that hinder us from being changed into the image of God and thereby receiving our inheritance as a part of His family. We must conquer them in order to experience the love of God in the family of God. Contention, jealousy, outbursts of wrath, selfishness, ambitions, desires to rule, dissensions, heresies, envy, murder, drunkenness, and the like are all "ites" that keep us from our inheritance. (See Galatians 5:19–21.)

To run out the "ites" means to run out all forms of adultery as well, which is carrying on an affair with your own flesh as well as with someone who does not belong to you. All fornication, uncleanness, hatred, and unforgiveness must be purged from these temples of the Holy Ghost so that Christ may receive glory in the church, His body.

God's church will march triumphantly into her inheritance. Do you think Jesus will be hindered from having what the Father planned? The church is going to follow the example of Joshua and destroy the "ites," which are enemies that keep us from possessing our inheritance.

I thought that was the end of the message, but it wasn't. Some time later, my Teacher whispered to me that He wanted me to go back and read that passage in Joshua again, because I had not seen everything He wanted me to see. He told me to look to see *when* Joshua was going into the land. I read, "Pass through the host, and command the people, saying, Prepare you victuals; for within three days ye shall pass over this Jordan, to go in to possess the land, which the LORD your God giveth you to possess it" (Josh. 1:11).

God commanded Joshua to prepare the people, for in *three days* they were going to enter the land.

In Scripture, the word *day* can refer to twenty-four hours or to an era of time. Peter wrote, "But, beloved, be not ignorant of this one thing, that one day is with the Lord as a thousand years, and a thousand years as one day" (2 Pet. 3:8).

If we apply that principle to our calendar, we would say that in the year 2000 our second "day" is coming to a close, and we are about to enter the "third day" of our age. Our calendar is based on the history of the church, with the year A.D. 1 beginning after Christ's resurrection.

It is quite exciting to follow the mention of the "third day" throughout the Bible. For example, Esther went before the king on the third day of prayer and fasting to plead with him to save her and her people, and Haman was hanged on the gallows prepared for Mordecai. On the third day, Jesus turned the water into wine at the wedding of Cana.

And before He died, He said, "Destroy this temple, and I will raise it again in three days" (John 2:19, NIV). The Jews thought He meant Solomon's Temple, and we have thought He meant His own body. But He didn't build His own body—He is building the church. He is the Head of the church, which is His body.

In the Book of Hosea, the prophet spoke regarding the third day:

> Come, and let us return unto the LORD: for he hath torn, and he will heal us; he hath smitten, and he will bind us up. After two days will he revive us: in the third day he will raise us up, and we shall live in his sight. Then shall we know, if we follow on to know the LORD: his going forth is prepared as the morning; and he shall come unto us as the rain, as the latter and former rain unto the earth.
>
> —Hosea 6:1–3

People who are hearing the voice of God know that He is going to do something soon. I said, "Now, Lord, don't let me go out into left field by projecting a timetable for Your moving."

I don't know how long the third day is going to last, but the church is getting ready to enter the third day. Every time we write the date we are affirming that the second day is coming to a close on our calendar. And we know the church is going into her inheritance, for Scripture teaches that Jesus is coming for a glorious church without spot or wrinkle.

We must become that church without spot or blemish, one mature man growing up into our

Head, which is Christ. Relating to the typology of Joshua, we must possess the land, conquering all the enemies of our souls, following our heavenly Joshua's battle plans, until we enter into all of our inheritance.

Some time after receiving this message of the Joshua generation and sharing it with the graduating class at Fountaingate, I was invited to speak to the youth who attended a large youth festival to be held on the hills of Front Royal, Virginia. The day I was to speak it was raining, and many of the seventeen thousand young people dressed in black garbage bags. Standing there in the rain, they listened intently as I shared with them God's plan for the Joshua generation. When I finished explaining how they could go into the inheritance God had planned for the church, I challenged them to answer the question, "Will you be part of the Joshua generation?"

A thunderous sound of youthful voices filled the air as they shouted, "We are, and we will be that Joshua generation."

It was an awesome sight to experience so many young people declaring their loyalty to Christ and His church. ◡

Twelve

A Mandate to Go to the
Body of Christ
❧

D
R. SUE CURRAN, pastor of Shekinah Church
Ministries in Blountville, Tennessee, was one
of my peers with a prophetic mantle who sensed that
God was releasing me from pastoring to go to the
body of Christ at large. She came to me and said
simply, "Fuchsia, if you ever decide to leave
Fountaingate, my husband and I would like to invite
you and Leroy to make your home in Blountville,
Tennessee, with us."

WEEPING COMES BEFORE JOY

MANY OF MY peers in ministry, as well as prophets to
the body of Christ and those in my lovely congregation, were confirming the word of the Lord. He was
sending me as a "mother in Israel" to the body of

Christ, to look for leaders and teach them to train the body of Christ to go in and possess the land that had never been possessed by the church.

Though I sensed a major change was coming, I knew that the God who spoke to Mary was the same one who gave instructions to Joseph. So without discussing with my husband the invitation I had received from Pastor Curran, I waited for God's confirmation.

One day at lunch my husband, Leroy, said to me, "Honey, when we move to Tennessee, this workshop will be a job to pack, won't it?" He had a shop in a room of our home. He continued, "Do you think I ought to start packing it up soon?"

I looked at him, startled by his question. "Well, I think that would be a good idea, honey," I replied. There was no further discussion of our decision. We both knew we were being led of God into this change.

In 1988, our church followed the leading of our Lord to thrust us out into the field to the body of Christ. Once again, faith was tested as we left the security of friends and home to trust God for His provision in every area of our lives. Under a new mandate, we sold our home and moved to Kingsport, Tennessee, to establish our residence and to make Shekinah Church Ministries of Blountville, Tennessee, our home church.

Shekinah was not new to us, for we had enjoyed ministering in their conferences and had been a part of their wonderful ministerial fellowship for many years. They graciously offered us office facilities, and we began to travel out from Tennessee, with this church as our headquarters and base of operations.

It was with great anticipation that my husband and I began a new phase of ministry, though not without some reservations. Did the body of Christ really need us? Would the message we had be accepted? We would soon know the answer to those questions as we followed in obedience to our God on the pathway He was opening for us. And fresh revelation was still coming to my heart as my Teacher continued to unfold His present-day purposes for His church.

BODY OF CHRIST TORN

As I BEGAN to receive invitations to travel throughout the body of Christ, my heart became more and more heavy-laden. I did not see glimmers of revival as I had hoped. Instead, I saw the body of Christ being attacked and torn by at least five major enemies. As I wrote in my book, *The Next Move of God*, there were at least five enemies that were trying to destroy the body of Christ: the Jezebel spirit, the Absalom spirit, the Pharisaical spirit, the witchcraft spirit, and the pseudo-counseling spirit.

As I ministered in different churches each week, I met ministers who would stay at the lunch table with me for three or four hours talking about what God was doing in the earth. They were hungry to see God move, and they would weep and say, "I have heard something that God wants to do. It is wonderful. Am I crazy?"

Many of them were being given the left foot of fellowship by their denominations.

And I would get so excited I could hardly contain myself. I knew they were connected to that power plant—they were being filled with the water that would run one day to the nations. And I would say to each of them, "You are hearing correctly. Don't worry about denominations. Don't worry about what they think. You are moving toward the next move of God."

These enemies were advocates of the *CODE*—the religious order of the day that would not give way to the new thing God was doing. The *CODE* is a word the Holy Spirit gave me recently to summarize the five things that hinder the move of God—prejudice, tradition, denominationalism, custom, and culture. The *CODE* is what killed Jesus. It is what keeps women from preaching. It is what separates and divides the body of Christ over nonessentials. The religious world has established a code. The more I traveled, the more I encountered the terrible effects of the code, and I wondered what had happened to the revival I was expecting.

Years earlier, after I received the vision of the hydroelectric power plant and heard the waters rolling, understanding what God was going to do in the church age, I geared my life for the day that vision would be fulfilled. That revelation became a frame of reference for my life, and I wanted to train students to get ready for the wonderful revival that was coming. Great desire filled my heart for that revival.

I didn't know that it was going to be called *revival*. But I wanted the great breakthrough of the Word of God that I had seen in the analogy of the river flowing into that power plant. From that day on, that river has been real to me. I have heard that water in churches where I have ministered. But I began to realize that we would have to go outside the walls of denominationalism to hear the waters of revival.

RESTORATION OF NAOMI

ONE OF MY annual invitations is to participate in a tremendous family camp at Blue Mountain Christian Retreat in New Ringgold, Pennyslvania. It is always a delightful time of ministry that I share as guest speaker along with my pastor, Sue Curran. We have seen lives changed by the power of God as these hungry people come to receive from the ministry of the Word.

One evening, as I was ministering there, God gave me new understanding of the Book of Ruth.[1] Though I had received wonderful revelation of this allegory, in that moment as I was teaching I began to see something new unfold as part of God's purpose for the church.

The Holy Spirit had already shown me the restoration of the church in the type of Ruth, the Moabitess. I was thrilled with this understanding that the church would be redeemed and receive her inheritance much as Ruth did. But suddenly, as I ministered these truths under the anointing, the Holy Spirit flashed an understanding to my mind of Naomi. Not only was Ruth redeemed, but Naomi was fully restored to her inheritance as well.

In that moment I understood that Naomi, a type of the denominational church, would have the baby son placed into her arms by Ruth, receiving her inheritance along with Ruth's redemption.

Naomi had left the presence of God in the land of Bethlehem-judah and had returned in bitterness of soul, having lost all that was precious to her in the land of Moab. She had no inheritance, no joy, no future as a widow in a foreign land.

But when she returned to the "house of bread" (the translation of Bethlehem-judah), the Lord surprised her by restoring her to inheritance through her Moabitish daughter-in-law. She had learned that there was bread there once again, and she turned her steps homeward. When Ruth sought her mother-in-law's welfare as well as her own, Boaz honored her and eventually redeemed her completely, along with her mother-in-law. This is what is happening to the denominational people of today.

Why did God begin to bring laughter and joy back to the church in this present refreshing? Why have some laughed and rejoiced in the recent refreshing? Naomi had lost her "joy" and her "song" (translations of the names of her two sons, Mahlon and Chilion, who died in Moab). Her joy was restored when she returned to Bethlehem-judah and experienced restoration through the union of Boaz and Ruth.

Naomi did not know she was going to be restored to her inheritance. She knew she could go back to the land of bread. She was willing for her daughter-in-law to glean. But Naomi also knew who Boaz was. She didn't know he would do any thing for her, but she directed Ruth to the bridegroom and gave her instructions as to how to be brought to him. And because Ruth was restored through the wedding, Boaz cared for Naomi, too; he gave her the privilege of nurturing the life of the son.

This next move of God is going to see denominational people enjoying restoration along with the

"Ruths" who have found Boaz—their bridegroom-redeemer. And the glory of God is going to be revealed throughout the church as we continue to walk the pathway our Lord walked, following the pattern Son to the Mount of Transfiguration.

GOING TO THE MOUNT OF TRANSFIGURATION

RECENTLY THE HOLY Spirit spoke to me about the transfiguration of Jesus. I wrote about what He revealed to me in my book, *Receiving Divine Revelation*, and I want to share a portion of that revelation in this book.[2]

I understood that God intends for believers to follow the pattern Son through the seven steps of redemption Christ walked while on earth. We are first to receive Christ's divine life by being born again; next, we are to be water baptized; and third, we are to experience the baptism of the Holy Spirit.

The fourth step of redemption is to be led into the wilderness as Jesus was to overcome the enemy of our souls, defeating him as Jesus did when He declared, "It is written" (Matt. 4:4). Our wildernesses may take many forms—having to leave our relatives, friends, doctrinal positions, ambitions, or plans to follow Christ. We can all testify to a place of temptation where we have had to establish our determination to worship God alone.

But how many of us have thought of the next step in Jesus' life, that which took Him to the Mount of Transfiguration? It was there that He experienced the supernatural unveiling of the glory of God and heard the voice from heaven that once again affirmed, "This is my beloved Son, in whom I am well pleased" (Matt. 17:5). Surely a similar experience does not occur in the lives of believers.

We understand that we will be required to go to the cross to be crucified with Christ in order to enjoy resurrection power. Thus, of the seven steps of redemption, all but the fifth one, being transfigured, seem easy to apply to the life of the believer.

As I was meditating on the Scriptures, the Holy Spirit showed me that what was revealed in the transfiguration of Jesus was Adam as he would have become if he had not fallen. He would have become a mature son of God who pleased the Father in all that he did.

The Scriptures refer to Christ as the last Adam (1 Cor. 15:45). As Christ grew in favor with God and man and did His Father's will, He became the mature Son whom the Father could affirm. It was then that He entered into the ministry God had ordained for Him, directed by the Holy Spirit. Everything He did on earth was by the power of the Holy Spirit working through His humanity.

As I continued meditating on the wonder of the transfiguration, the Holy Spirit directed me to the Book of Romans. He asked me what the word *transformed* meant in Romans 12:2. As I studied the word, I understood that it could be translated as "transfigured." It comes from the word *metamorphosis* and means "to be changed or metamorphosed."

I began to weep and tremble as I saw the truth God was making clear. In this verse the apostle Paul instructs us: "I beseech you therefore, brethren, by the mercies of God, that ye present your bodies a living sacrifice, holy, acceptable unto God, which is your reasonable service . . . be ye transformed by the renewing of your mind" (Rom. 12:1–2). What he is really saying is for us to be transfigured by the power of the Holy Spirit living within us.

How is God going to fill our temples with His glory? When we surrender our bodies to Him as living sacrifices we will become transfigured so the glory of God will be seen in us and shine forth through us. His Word, the living Word, working in us His good pleasure, will transform us so that the presence of God will shine forth from us. Then we will go forth in power, as Jesus did, to work the works of God that He has ordained for us to do.

THE RIVER AND THE NEW ANOINTING

SEVERAL YEARS AGO during this most recent renewal we have been experiencing, Olen Griffing, pastor of Shady Grove Church in Shady Grove, Texas, was invited to speak at the annual ministers' conference at Shekinah Ministries where we make our headquarters. We have ministered at this annual conference for many years and enjoy seeing God refresh and strengthen His servants year after year.

Pastor Griffing was giving his testimony of how God had begun to let him experience the river in his own life and in his church. Though he was at first skeptical of the manifestations such as falling and laughing, he had been swept into the "river" and was now enjoying a wonderful move of God in his church. The title of his message was, "Let God Be God," and he gave a call for ministers who wanted to surrender to whatever God wanted to do and become a part of His revival.

I don't know how I got to the altar—I cannot run

or even walk quickly without someone helping me because of my physical limitations due to osteo-porosis. But I was the first one there. Pastor Griffing and others began to pray for the ministers and con-ferees, and when he touched me, I fell—as did many others that night. I experienced some "carpet time" in the presence of the Lord. Lying there, I was oblivious to anyone else being there, though the sanctuary was full of conferees. As far as I was con-cerned, there wasn't a soul in the world in the church.

As I lay there, I began to see the most brilliant light I had ever seen. Though the word *brilliance* is perhaps the superlative word in my vocabulary, it wouldn't begin to describe this light. It was beyond comprehension or description. As I watched in fas-cination, I saw that light take the shape of a Person. And I knew it was Jesus. I didn't see what I saw years ago—the human Jesus with blue eyes and long flowing hair. This time I saw Him as *the* Light.

He was standing on the other side of the church in a doorway, and He beckoned for me to come to Him. He spoke these words, "Daughter, for thirty-two years you have listened for the river in churches all over the country. You won't have to listen only for the river anymore. Tonight I want you to come into the river. Come with Me."

I am not comfortable in water. I have never learned to swim. And because of my present physical condition I can't even lie on my back comfortably. Yet I was lying on the carpet that night on my back for almost two hours and never felt any ill effects. As I consented to the Lord to get into the river, even though I cannot swim physically, I began to swim and swim and swim in those wonderful waters.

Those who were with me that night said I moved my arms and did every gesture of swimming lying there on the carpet; I even "dog-paddled." All I was aware of was that wonderful river that was flowing from the throne of God. I was swimming with Jesus in the river. Since that experience, I have prayed for hundreds of people at a time and watched as they were baptized in that river of the wonderful presence of God.

Don't tell me the river is not here. God promised me I would live to see the revival come in and experience the deluge of water from that hydroelectric plant. That water is coming to the church now. The dam is not yet open, but it will come. The flood is not yet here, but the river is flowing.

A few weeks later, I went to The Carpenter's Home Church in Lakeland, Florida, to hear Rodney Howard-Browne minister. I had never seen him before. That is the only time I have ever seen him. I was sitting on the front row at the request of Pastor Strader. As Rodney Howard-Browne was ministering, he walked in front of me, pointed to me, and shouted, "The river is here."

I answered him, "I know it."

He looked at me again and repeated, "The river is here."

Three times he repeated that statement directly to me. I started swimming again. I almost fell off my seat.

I was preaching somewhere not too long ago, and I proclaimed, "The river is here."

Suddenly I grabbed the pulpit and thought, *Hang on, Fuchsia. You're going down again!*

Revelation is flowing in that river, the unveiling of

Jesus Christ. There is no telling what is going to happen when that river flows freely. We won't have to specialize in one little area of truth when that river comes.

When I heard that river and began to understand that the church would walk the same seven steps that Jesus did—including transfiguration—I saw that after the glory comes we will go back down the mountain as Jesus did and do the miracles He did. The world will see His glory in the church as Jesus prayed they would. (See John 17.)

Jesus didn't go to heaven from the Mount of Transfiguration—He went back down the mountain and cast out the demon that the disciples were not able to cast out.

In Ezekiel's vision of the river, he saw that it was full of fish. When it was flowing to its greatest depth, it carried a harvest of fish. We are going to see a wonderful ingathering of souls when that river begins to run unhindered with waters to swim in. We are simply awaiting the timing of God, allowing Him to fill us with His Word of truth, and yielding to the moving of the Holy Spirit as He begins to flow that river through us.

God has always moved according to His time-table. In the fullness of time He sent His Son. Jesus, our great Passover Lamb, was slain at the moment the lamb was being struck in the temple on the Day of Atonement. When the Day of Pentecost had fully come, He sent the Holy Spirit to indwell His church. He established feast days and has submitted all His dealings with mankind to a divine timetable.

Jesus told His disciples, "The harvest truly is plenteous, but the labourers are few; pray ye therefore the Lord of the harvest, that he will send forth labourers into his harvest" (Matt. 9:37–38). Our assignment is to be prepared to gather the great End-Time harvest that is coming. Our hearts must be prepared to be sent forth by the Lord of the Harvest, who is not willing that any should perish.

As Leroy and I have traveled continually these last ten years, the doors opened to us for ministry have been seemingly countless and the privileges glorious. The joy of ministry has continually been the blessed ministry of my Teacher—the blessed Holy Spirit—and I have seen many others come across the stones in the river as the church moves forward into her inheritance. ∾

Notes

CHAPTER ONE
MEMORIAL STONES

1. The seven-step process of revelation is discussed in detail in Fuchsia Pickett's book, *Receiving Divine Revelation* (Lake Mary, FL: Creation House, 1997), 98–102.

CHAPTER THREE
LONGING FOR RELATIONSHIP WITH GOD

1. "In the Garden" by Austin Miles. Copyright © 1912 by Hall-Mack. Renewed 1940 by The Rodeheaver Co. (A Div. of WORD MUSIC). All rights reserved. Used by permission.

CHAPTER NINE
INTRODUCTION TO WEST COAST MINISTRY

1. Fuchsia Pickett, *Presenting the Holy Spirit,* vols. 1 and 2 (Lake Mary, FL: Creation House, reprint 1997), 143–179.

CHAPTER TEN
REVIVAL AND REVELATION

1. Patrick Alexander, Stanley M. Burgess, and Gary B. McGee, *Dictionary of Pentecostal and Charismatic Movements* (Grand Rapids, MI: Zondervan, 1988), s.v. Beal, Myrtle D.

2. Fuchsia Pickett, *The Next Move of God* (Lake Mary, FL: Creation House, 1996), 9–10. In this book Fuchsia Pickett recounts her vision of the hydroelectric power plant in detail.

Notes

CHAPTER ELEVEN
A NEW NAME

1. Fuchsia Pickett, *God's Dream* (Shippensburg, PA: Destiny Image Publishers, 1991), 121–140. In *God's Dream*, Fuchsia Pickett related how the Holy Spirit answered her request for a life-changing message for the graduating class at Fountaingate Bible College. The description of God's message to her as written in this book is adapted from her book, *God's Dream*.

CHAPTER TWELVE
A MANDATE TO GO TO THE BODY OF CHRIST

1. Fuchsia Pickett, *The Prophetic Romance* (Lake Mary, FL: Creation House, 1996). This book by Fuchsia Pickett describes in detail her revelation of the Book of Ruth.

2. Portions of chapter 12 have been adapted from Fuchsia Pickett's book, *Receiving Divine Revelation*, 155–157.